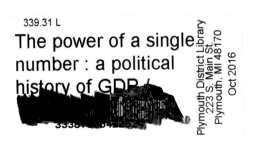

THE POWER OF A SINGLE NUMBER

THE
POWER
OF A
SINGLE
NUMBER

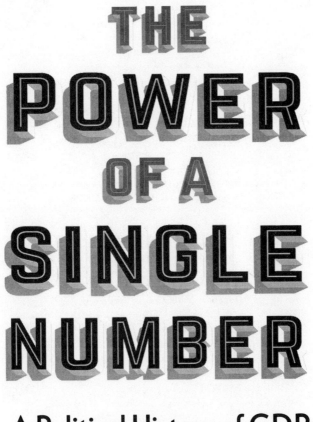

A Political History of GDP

PHILIPP LEPENIES

TRANSLATED BY JEREMY GAINES

COLUMBIA UNIVERSITY PRESS | NEW YORK

Columbia University Press
Publishers Since 1893
New York   Chichester, West Sussex
Die Macht der einen Zahl: Eine politische Geschichte des
Bruttoinlandsprodukts © 2013 Suhrkamp Verlag Berlin
English translation © 2016 Columbia University Press

The English translation of this text was financed by a grant from the
Institute for Advanced Sustainablity Studies (IASS), Potsdam.

Library of Congress Cataloging-in-Publication Data

Names: Lepenies, Philipp, 1971– author.
Title: The power of a single number : a political history of GDP /
Philipp Lepenies ; translated by Jeremy Gaines.
Other titles: Macht der einen Zahl. English
Description: New York : Columbia University Press, 2016. | Includes biblio-
graphical references and index.
Identifiers: LCCN 2015034785 | ISBN 9780231175104 (cloth : alk. paper) |
ISBN 9780231541435 (e-book)
Subjects: LCSH: Gross domestic product—Political aspects—History.
Classification: LCC HC79.15 L4613 2016 | DDC 339.3/109—dc23
LC record available at http://lccn.loc.gov/2015034785

Cover design by Noah Arlow.

paralleled with a grant
Figure Foundation

CONTENTS

INTRODUCTION

Gross domestic product (GDP) is the most powerful statistical figure in human history. No other indicator has ever had such an impact. At first glance, GDP is simply the measure of a country's economic output, the value of all goods and services produced in a specific period, expressed as a number. However, GDP is far more than a mere statistic. Together with growth, which describes its rate of change, GDP serves as the key indicator of development and progress. Positive GDP growth is both the express objective of almost all governments and is often considered the only possible way out of an economic crisis. The global economy and global politics are largely defined by GDP.

Yet, GDP is not a self-explanatory figure like the temperature in Fahrenheit, last year's CO_2 emissions in tons, or the total calories of your breakfast. Instead, it is a calculation method that includes certain economic aspects but excludes others. It relies on a convention, on one interpretation of what we understand output and the economy to be.

GDP is a unique metric: economic activities are translated into numbers, added up according to predetermined rules, and aggregated as a single money value. In reality, this quite literally and most emphatically is a matter of *political arithmetic*: GDP is not only calculated on behalf of the government; it also feeds back into government actions. It enables governing by numbers.

For the U.S. Department of Commerce, GDP counts as one of the "greatest inventions of the twentieth century,"[1] although others have long been suspicious of the power it exerts. For example, former French president Nicolas Sarkozy wrote, in the foreword to the report published by the commission he set up to measure economic performance and social progress, "We have wound up mistaking our representations of wealth for the wealth itself, and our representations of reality for the reality itself. . . . We have built a cult of the data, and we are now enclosed within."[2] On the one side, there are those who vilify GDP and the exclusive focus on growth, while, on the other, there are the advocates who, at most, would accept slight tweaks to the methodology for measuring GDP, but otherwise continue to sing their high praise for growth. However, on both sides there is no doubt that GDP is of central importance to our political culture.

How did it come about that GDP now has such powers? How could a statistical construct that was completely unknown before World War II triumph over all else? These are the kind of questions this book sets out to answer. It traces the history of GDP—or, to be precise, the genesis and onward march of the idea of the gross national product (GNP) and, to a certain extent, the older idea of national income. In the 1990s, GDP replaced the concept of gross national product, customarily used since the end of World War II as the key economic and political statistical indicator. The variables differ only in the details, which are of subordinate importance here. For this reason, I shall simplify and refer mostly to GDP, although historically speaking, it would be more accurate to use the term gross national product.

GDP's special position results from its political acceptance. For this reason, it is crucial to identify the point in time and the circumstances that led to the recognition of gross national product as a meaningful "technology of government" and then the definitive emergence of its calculation as a matter of political arithmetic.[3]

This book does not seek to offer a comprehensive history of national accounts, as that has already been written by others.[4] It focuses instead on the political contexts in which GDP arose and the decisive episodes in which it gained sway. This will better allow us to grasp the unique complexity of that history, the traditions on which GDP is based, and the precursors to it. The starting point here is not only the astonishment that Sarkozy expresses, at the power that GDP exerts today, but, above all, the lack of this historical perspective in current attempts to change it, supplement it, or even topple it, as many wish.

Three people play key roles in the political history of GDP: William Petty, Colin Clark, and Simon Kuznets. Petty's attempts, in seventeenth-century England, to transform naked figures into politically relevant data and thus into an instrument of power (a political arithmetic) constitutes an important historical precursor to GDP. Clark was an ingenious lone wolf, an English chemist who, after the Great Depression, was frustrated by the lack of macro-economic data and who, working on his own, laid many of the foundations for the calculation of GDP. Kuznets was born in Russia and relied on his experiences in the early days of the Soviet Union to produce a systematic calculation of national accounts; he did this at the same time as Clark, with the signal difference that Kuznets's work was explicitly commissioned by government.

No one doubts the importance of Petty, Clark, and Kuznets. Yet, there is a touch of tragedy about the role they played; despite their importance to the history of GDP, none succeeded in convincing others of their methodologies during their lifetimes. The history of GDP is also an object lesson in the circumstances under which ideas can have political effect. Ideologies exerted an influence here, as did extreme events such as the Great Depression and World War II. And without John Maynard Keynes, who drew heavily on the work of both Clark and Kuznets, the history of GDP would have been very different.

The complex history of GDP shows how the number gained such an incredible power and the reasons for its triumph: namely, GDP proved itself in times of crisis, emerged as an international norm, and rested on a belief in the utility of political arithmetic. And the history of the measure, above all, makes it clear that the notion of GDP and the ideal of growth is aligned to a set of political values that were originally intended to solve the problems of war and of the immediate postwar years.

I shall start this study by defining a few of the important technical terms, such as GDP, gross national product, and national income. Readers who are more familiar with economics may wish to skip this chapter. However, it is no doubt advantageous to remind oneself of these foundations. I shall then present William Petty and his idea of political arithmetic. Colin Clark and the case of England are the topic addressed in the third chapter; Simon Kuznets and that of the United States in the fourth. In the fifth chapter, the focus turns to Germany, and the final chapter addresses how the idea of growth and of a gross national product eventually spawned the dogma of growth—and how the powers of the single number reached a peak.

Why Germany, of all places? Why not other countries as examples? I would suggest that there are few countries in the Western world where economic growth and the related forms of arithmetic have played as great a role, during the second half of the twentieth century, as they did in Germany. The "economic miracle," meaning the country's swift economic recovery after the destruction of World War II, measured in terms of gross national and later gross domestic product, was a founding narrative of the young republic. It seemed almost as if the dark historical epoch of the Third Reich, the war, and all the misery it had caused could be erased from memory by showing, by means of manifest economic prosperity, that the country was in a radical process of modernization, that a new era had started. In no other country (other than the United States) did economic success become such a fetish, did the faith in economic growth get celebrated almost religiously, as it did in Germany. Postwar Germany and growth in gross national product went hand in hand.

Popular culture shows just how strongly statistical deno-tation of economic power can shape the consciousness of an entire country, such as Germany. How else can one explain that, in 1983, a relatively unknown band called Geier Sturzflug (Vulture's Nosedive) managed to land a number one hit single for several weeks in a row, titled, quite unromantically, "Bruttosozialprodukt"—"Gross National Product"? The song's refrain, which most Germans still know well enough to sing along to, goes, "Ja, jetzt wird wieder in die Hände gespuckt / Wir steigern das Bruttosozialprodukt" (Now let's get down to work / Let's boost the gross national product). Even if the song was meant ironically and hit the charts during a period of high unemployment, it is a telling indication of the high status German society attaches to the benchmark.

There are, however, additional reasons for taking a closer look at the case of Germany. The success of gross domestic product as a yardstick with a fixed place in politics is actually a global success story. It is decisive here to remember just how the idea and method of GDP were exported. A political history of the gross domestic product can therefore only be written and grasped in terms of its transnational historiography. It is not just the countries and the contexts in which GDP arose that have to be considered, but also the processes and circumstances through which it asserted itself in other countries. One could, of course, study many other, different countries, but Germany seems especially suitable, particularly because the political success of GDP in the United States was closely bound up with the goal of winning the war against Germany. It is all the more interesting, therefore, to see how this method finally gained sway in precisely the country it was originally invented to destroy.

THE POWER OF A SINGLE NUMBER

1

WHAT IT'S ALL ABOUT

A Short Primer on GDP

In conceptual terms, gross domestic product is a product, although in mathematical terms it is actually a sum total. The idea of GDP is based on the supposition that one can grasp all the goods produced and services provided in a country as a single aggregated asset, the monetary value of which can be calculated. That also explains why the term is used in the singular and one never talks of a country's "gross domestic products."

The simplest definition of GDP is that it is the "value of the total domestic economic output of a particular country's economy over a specific period."[1] It refers to all "goods produced and services provided domestically (value added), inasmuch as these do not take the form of inputs for the manufacture of other goods and services."[2]

Here, "value" simply means monetary units. It is not quantities or the quality of products or services that are relevant for GDP, but the accumulated price of all goods produced. It is, however, not the final market price of, for example, a car that is recorded, but only the value that the automobile manufacturer, as the last in the production chain, adds. The value of all the inputs the car manufacturer made use of to produce the car (commodities, services, or intermediate products, the so-called intermediate consumption) must be deducted from the price of the vehicle. This avoids cases of double counting, as the value of the inputs has already been charged and recorded by the particular producers, be it the tire manufacturer or the tanner who provides the leather seats for the car.[3]

A valuation on the basis of prices implies that only goods and services that are traded on the market are included in the calculation. Goods and services provided without a market price attached to them are of no significance for GDP. These include, for example, unpaid housework or the use of natural resources, which from the point of view of market logic are available free of charge.

"Growth" is determined by the rate of change in GDP from one period to another. It is expressed as a percentage and is price adjusted, meaning an attempt is made to exclude inflation. Otherwise, a mere rise in price would appear to be growth in GDP, even if there had been no increase at all in the volume of goods produced or services rendered.[4]

"Gross" means that the decline in value of the utilized capital during the production process (in particular the wear and tear on the machines) is not taken into account. Should this value impairment be calculated in the form of depreciation, the gross domestic product would become the net domestic product.

We speak of the *domestic* product because only the economic activities performed by individuals in a specific economic area (frequently, within the borders of a particular nation-state) are factored into the calculation ("domestic concept"). The individuals' nationality and domicile play no role whatever. The value added of a Chinese company producing in the United States is just as much included in the GDP of the United States as the work of a commuter who travels from Canada to his workplace across the border. However, GDP does not include the value added of an American company producing in the People's Republic of China, nor the income of an employee who lives in Detroit and works in Canada.

In terms of how it is computed, gross national product (GNP) is basically identical to GDP (here, again, the focus is on the sum total of value added). The important difference is that gross national product is based not on a concept of what is "domestic" but on a notion of what is "national" ("national concept"). In other words, gross national product records the value added achieved by all the people permanently domiciled in a specific country, regardless of whether this is achieved within the boundaries of the country in which they live, in neighboring countries, or in other parts of the world.

Increasing globalization has made it even more important to determine the economic output generated by a country within its own territory. This data—which GDP provides— seems more informative than gross national product for short-term analyses of a country's economic situation. For this reason, in 1991 the United States altered its method of calculation, from gross national product to GDP; in Germany, the switch took place six years later.

The method of calculating GDP (and this also applies to gross national product) is special because GDP can be determined in three different ways. By definition, the results of all three approaches must concur, and thus the value of GDP can be verified in various ways, making the calculated figure more coherent and plausible.

GDP is calculated by focusing on production ("production output"), on expenditure ("expenditure approach"), or on income ("income approach"). With regard to production, GDP is calculated using producers' gross value added, as described above. By contrast, the expenditure approach highlights what end consumers spend on goods and services—that is, the value of the goods and services they procure through the market. This approach focuses on the demand side. Private consumer spending, government expenditure, gross capital formation, and exports are added up, and the value of imports (or what is known as the balance of trade) is deducted. This method of calculation also results in GDP.

The third method of calculation, the income approach, is based on totaling up the income generated by the production process during the period under review. This involves first aggregating employee compensation (in accordance with the national concept) and adding it to corporate income and property income. This produces the national income, which is also referred to as the "net national income at factor cost." Put simply, it is the sum total of the income available to the people living in a particular economy.

Adding to this figure depreciation and taxes and duties on production and imports, while subtracting state subsidies, we arrive at gross national income. It is arithmetically identical to gross national product but is calculated via the income side.[5] If we then deduct from the so-called primary income, which is received from or paid to the rest of the world (and includes labor income and interest received), the national concept becomes the domestic concept, and the amount calculated in turn corresponds to GDP.

In Germany, GDP calculation is based only on production and expenditure. There is a lack of data relating to property and entrepreneurial income, and this prevents GDP from being computed from the income side. Instead, the data is calculated as a residual value.[6]

GDP and the way it is calculated are part of what is known as national accounts. They are intended to provide "as comprehensive and comprehensible a picture as possible of the economic activities" of a country.[7] It is a system of accounts and tables that express, in figures, the course of the economy and the economic activities of people and institutions. Only by using these accounts and tables can GDP be calculated at all.

National accounts are based on a system of double-entry bookkeeping: a change in assets (use) on one side must correspond to a change in liabilities (resources) entered on the other. The data are compiled by drawing on current surveys of economic statistics, business statistics, the annual financial statements of major corporations, surveys of private households, and information from industry associations. The calculation of GDP represents the most prominent section of national accounts. The other sections include input/output calculations, national wealth accounts, and employment accounts.

The method of determining GDP by means of national accounts is harmonized internationally. In the European Union, the European System of Accounts (ESA), dating from 2010, applies; this largely concurs with the United Nations' 2008 System of National Accounts (SNA), which is used worldwide. National accounts are part of official statistics, the compilation of which is a public duty of each sovereign nation, and for this reason is conducted by public agencies.

National accounts enable us to get a picture of the interrelations among all economically active people in a society. Economics textbooks often begin with a graphic representation of the economic cycle. At its simplest, it comprises the relationship between companies (the economy) and the working population (if, for simplicity's sake, we exclude the state as an actor and cross-border trade). The cycle is described vividly in the form of two currents, flowing in different directions, between the economy and the population. One current represents the productive side of the economy: the workforce provides companies with manpower, which producers use to create goods and services, which in turn are consumed by the population. The current moving in the other direction describes monetary flows: companies pay employees wages and salaries for the work they perform, which employees in turn use to acquire goods and services from the companies. These currents are visualized and quantified in the production, expenditure, and income approaches of calculating GDP. GDP is the pooled, aggregated variable moving in one or the other direction along the relevant trajectories of the economic cycle.

Despite the different methods of calculation (production, expenditure, or income distribution), GDP is primarily a measure of production. For this reason, growth—the rate of change in GDP—is also primarily defined as an increase in production. For decades, the criticism leveled against the idea of GDP and growth has been that GDP has do with goods, and growth implies an increase in production. In other words, GDP is a materialistic concept.

It was of historic significance when, in the prevailing political mind-set, gross national product (as the precursor of GDP) and a focus on production replaced the older idea of national income based on income flows. Only when the focus shifted from income distribution to produced goods did the concept of GDP become politically relevant. With the focus on production, a statistical construct became a matter of politics; gross national product became the single most powerful political number. At the same time, gross national product became a tool intended to achieve far more than mere expansion of the volume of goods and services. The success of gross national product and GDP is based on the fact that, with them, politicians were from the outset able to pursue a whole array of goals beyond just documenting economic processes.

2

WILLIAM PETTY AND POLITICAL ARITHMETIC

The Origins of GDP

Englishman William Petty (1623–1687) is regarded as the first person to consider the idea of calculating national income. He was a jack-of-all-trades: a physician, music professor, statistician, member of Parliament, demographer, cartographer, industrialist, and author. London's famed chronicler Samuel Pepys wrote of Petty that he was "the most rational man that ever he heard speak with a tongue."[1]

Recording existing wealth or tax revenue has always been an important administrative task for any ruler—regardless of whether the territory was a small duchy or a large empire. Petty, however, was one of the first to recognize that the combination and interpretation of certain empirically calculable or estimated data could indicate that the state should act in a certain way. He called his method political arithmetic, and he was aware that it was a source of power not only for the state itself but also for those who conducted this arithmetic.

As is characteristic of the entire history of the calculation of gross domestic product, Petty's deliberations were in response to a major political crisis. When, in the mid-seventeenth century, he was pondering how to accurately calculate national income, one of the "most dramatic and turbulent periods" in English history had just begun.[2] From 1642 until 1649, a civil war raged, culminating in the establishment of a republic under Oliver Cromwell. During the Glorious Revolution of 1688, England was attacked by Holland, and King James II was overthrown. Scotland and Ireland experienced internal, armed conflicts. There was war with France, and on top of that, outbreaks of hunger and plague epidemics. No other century in all of English history has witnessed such political turmoil.

WILLIAM PETTY AND POLITICAL ARITHMETIC

Petty was born in humble circumstances in 1623, in Hampshire. At the age of fourteen he went to sea, but his extreme shortsightedness proved to be his downfall: Once, while on watch, he overlooked a sandbar and the ship ran aground. By order of the captain he was flogged, and his arm was broken. Unfit for further maritime service, the boy was left behind on the Normandy coast, injured and alone. Petty made his way to Caen, where he so impressed the Jesuits teaching there that they allowed him to enroll at their university. He subsequently returned to England, only to flee, in 1643, from the civil war that had broken out. He studied medicine in Utrecht, Leiden, Amsterdam, and Paris, where for a short while he assisted Thomas Hobbes and got to know Descartes.[3]

As a young anatomist at Oxford, in 1650, while giving a lecture at the dissecting table, he succeeded in resuscitating the supposed corpse of a young woman who had been hung but had not died. The short treatise, *News from the Dead*, which went into circulation shortly afterwards and offered a sensationalist account of the incident, suddenly made Petty famous, and it gave him his first professorship, which was later be followed by a chair in music.[4]

Petty left the university in 1652, having enlisted as a physician in Cromwell's army. He served in Ireland, where, with the Irish rebellion (1641–1651) crushed, large swathes of the country were divided up among the English occupying forces. As a result, a land register and the first exact map of the island were required. Thanks to his organizational skills and his specialist knowledge, Petty very quickly conducted this mapping process, thereby making a name for himself in England's political circles. With the help of his map, land and estates were divided up and the local population was driven out. Under dubious circumstances, Petty also became one of Ireland's biggest landowners and, as a result, had to contend with political hostility for the rest of his life. As an ennobled member of Parliament, he vehemently defended the interest of the English settlers in Ireland.

Petty was a member of an informal association of scholars in London who concerned themselves closely with the experimental natural sciences. The findings and ideas of Francis Bacon were a pivotal influence on them. Bacon assumed that induction, empiricism, and experiments help us understand nature, and thus improve humanity's lot. This new method would prompt a total renewal of knowledge, he suggested, bringing about an *"instauratio magna"*—which was also the title of his uncompleted main philosophical work. The revolution through knowledge was closely bound up with the idea that applying the new method would put humankind in a position to change the world in which it lived, to influence nature, and thus to finally establish human rule on earth.[5]

The Bacon dictum "knowledge is power" referred to the authority of the state. Authority based on knowledge would, he thought, enable the regent to secure and extend his dominion. The production of knowledge was therefore at least as important as the best weapon, or as a battle that had been won.

In 1662, this loosely knit group gave birth to the Royal Society, with Petty himself, as one of its founding members, inventing several machines, including a large catamaran intended to revolutionize maritime trade. However, the ship, christened the *Experiment*, was never actually built, as the prototype sank while being demonstrated.

Also in 1662, Petty helped his friend John Graunt write the treatise *Natural and Political Observations Made upon the Bills of Mortality*, which is considered to be the very first publication on statistics. Using the mortality tables compiled weekly in London, the two men endeavored to analyze and interpret the available figures.[6] They deliberately used the word *political* in the title, because evaluation of the available data was intended to serve political and not purely academic purposes. The analysis of the mortality tables was politically significant for the simple reason that, with their help, the government was able to get an exact idea of how many men could be called up as soldiers in the event of war. The number of subjects provided information about the strength and wealth of a country, and was important for planning purposes.

Natural and Political Observations not only offered a detailed evaluation of the causes of death and the spread of specific illnesses and their causes; it also provided what, for the times, was a comprehensive picture of social and economic conditions. Furthermore, the authors made firm proposals about how data gathering could be improved and explained why further, ongoing statistical surveys would be meaningful.[7] They were surprised by how many people in the country did not work or were engaged in what, in the authors' eyes, were unnecessary activities. To their minds, these also included academics who addressed theological and philosophical speculations rather than focusing on nature and the material world, or who at best explored such mundane topics with words rather than with numbers and figures. A precise knowledge of a country's social and economic conditions was, they said, imperative "in order to good, certain, and easie [sic] Government." The art of governing, of "politicks," involved keeping the subjects in "peace and plenty."[8]

From the outset, the new scholarly methods were also applied to social processes. Bacon had compared a country's politics with the human body. Successful government therefore presupposed knowledge about how the body worked. For Petty the physician, this made sense: he circumspectly entitled the book he wrote in the 1660s, during the war against Holland, *The Political Anatomy of Ireland*.

Petty wrote a short article that was published in 1691 as an appendix to *Political Anatomy*. Its title was *"Verbum Sapienti"*—"A Word to the Wise [Is Sufficient]"—as if his expositions were to do with things that, for those in the know, required no further explanation. The subtitle was "An Account of the Wealth and Expences of England and the Method of raising Taxes in the most Equal manner. Shewing also, that the Nation can bear the charge of Four Millions per Annum, when the occasions of the Government require it."[9] The brief essay contained the first systematic calculation of national income.

Petty calculated the kingdom's national income ("annual proceeds") by estimating consumption ("expence of the nation"). By means of an assumed figure for daily per capita expenditure (for food, lodging, clothing, and other necessities), and on the basis of an estimated population of six million, he calculated a total figure for expenditure or consumption of £40 million per year. If the people of England were able to spend this amount in order to survive, then they must have income of the same magnitude. Petty calculated—or to be more precise, maintained—that the existing wealth, particularly property, only generated annual income of £15 million. The remaining £25 million, therefore, had to be explained by another source of income; namely, by the factor of labor. According to Petty, it was the income generated by wage labor that accounted for this figure.[10]

At first sight, the first crude calculation of national accounts looks trivial. Nor is the way it is presented particularly impressive. The results and calculations are explained in just a few lines, and only in writing. The underlying method, however, was totally new. Petty juxtaposed the income side with the expenditure side and broke both down into individual components. Furthermore, he made a rough distinction between stocks and flows because, in addition to income, he was also attempting to determine the value of existing assets.[11] His description allowed him to maintain that it was possible, using figures, to get a comprehensible idea of the structure and condition of a country's economic activities and to analyze how income is generated and spent.

Calculating national income was admittedly not an end in itself. Nor was an exact result decisive.[12] For Petty, being able to demonstrate with figures that a changed tax system would yield the Exchequer greater income than before was more important. The tax basis was far broader than had been assumed. In order to maintain this, however, Petty had to demonstrate credibly that only a small proportion of the income a country generated came from land ownership.[13] If the workforce was actually making a far larger contribution to income, it also could be successfully taxed. This was the decisive piece of information that Petty wanted to get across to politicians. He discovered the economic power of the working population. For this reason, Karl Marx and Friedrich Engels called him the "founder of modern political economics" and one of the "most ingenious and original economic researchers."[14] With the weight Petty attributed to labor in the economic process, he anticipated the labor theory of value, which was a cornerstone of the thought of both Adam Smith and Marx.

Unlike those active in the natural sciences, Petty was unable to rely on experiments or experimental setups for his calculations. Nonetheless, he was convinced that his approach was revolutionary: "The Method I take, is not yet very usual; for instead of using only comparative and superlative Words, and intellectual Arguments, I have taken the course (as a Specimen of the Political Arithmetick I have longed aimed at) to express my self in terms of Number, Weight, or Measure; to use only Arguments of Sense, and to consider only such Causes, as have visible Foundations in Nature."[15]

Petty's claim was staggering. With his method, he intended to replace theoretical observations and fantasies with an exact, measurable, quantifiable, and thus reliable picture of reality. Analyzing figures was a substitute for experiments. Figures describing social and economic phenomena were the result of actions by government. Studying the data enabled the success or failure of governmental measures to be evaluated, just as the results of experiments could be analyzed.

About a decade later, in 1676, Petty once again estimated England's national income. He entitled the essay in which he presented his calculations "Political Arithmetick." As the subtitle explained, it was "The Extent and Value of Lands, People, Buildings . . . &c. As the same relates to every Country in general, but more particularly to the Territories of His Majesty of Great Britain, and his Neighbours of Holland . . . and France." Petty compared his figures with statistics from the countries mentioned. He wanted to show that, on account of its wealth and resources, England, despite wars and revolution, was economically and militarily on a par with its two enemies. Given that the Crown intended to make England into a major European power, Petty's figures and deliberations were very opportune for the government.[16] The first essay on "Political Arithmetick," which would be followed by others with the same title, contained ten conclusions that Petty drew from his data analysis. He maintained, for example, that England's riches and power had proliferated in the previous forty years. For him, this was due not only to the increase in colonial territories and their economic exploitation but also to a massive improvement in infrastructure in the British Isles, to agricultural progress, and to trade expansion.[17] As another indication of increased affluence, Petty pointed to the tripling of the country's income during the same period. Basically, he opined, small countries could become as powerful and wealthy as wealthy ones if, on the back of the right policies, they succeeded in promoting trade and economic activity. In addition, Petty predicted that an improved tax system could result in the generation of sufficient revenue to finance a strong military power. More taxes could even lead to greater, instead of less, wealth.

Petty's conclusions were a dig at France. He stated that, given its natural and political circumstances, there was no way France could outdo England as a maritime power. Conversely, it was easily possible for England to draw level with France in terms of wealth and strength. Were the English Crown to impose a 10 percent tax on what the English spent, it could permanently maintain one hundred thousand foot soldiers, thirty thousand horses, and forty thousand sailors, and at the same time even build up reserves for unforeseeable situations. There were even enough workers and jobs available to increase the annual income generated in England by £2 million.

The essays penned under the title "Political Arithmetick" laid down the gauntlet. They were deliberately written to allay the English monarchy's fear of, and inferiority complex toward, a seemingly omnipotent, absolutist France that had regained its strength. Petty wanted to fire the politicians' hearts and illustrate that there was nothing standing in the way of England's greatness. With the data available Petty wanted to prove empirically that Great Britain could achieve more wealth and power.

The idea of a political arithmetic was politically explosive, not because of the figures but because of the interpretations, deductions, and political recommendations in which they resulted. Petty's writings initially circulated only in government circles and were regarded as secret. In France, where they nonetheless became known, Petty's theories caused considerable confusion. This may have been one of the reasons they were not published in England during Petty's lifetime. It was only after Petty's death that, with royal approval, his son, Lord Shelborne, released the essays (1690). The foreword reads, "Had not the Doctrins of this Essay offended France, they had long since seen the light, and had found Followers, as well as improvements before this time, to the advantage perhaps of Mankind."[18]

Lord Shelborne commented on the novelty of his father's methodic approach as follows: "It was by him stiled Political Arithmetick, in as much as things of Government, and of no less concern and extent, than the Glory of the Prince, and the happiness and greatness of the People, are by the Ordinary

Rules of Arithmetick, brought into a sort of Demonstration. He was allowed by all, to be the Inventor of this Method of Instruction; where the perplexed and intricate ways of the World, are explain'd by a very mean peice [sic] of Science."[19] So the political arithmetic was more than just figures. It could be used "to the advantage of mankind," and it visualized not only economic linkages but even the "perplexed and intricate ways of the World." Furthermore, the method increased the "Glory of the Prince" and the "happiness and greatness of the People": it enabled military power to be estimated and international comparisons to be made. The calculations Petty made in his *Political Arithmetick* were of significance far beyond the field of economics. In the essay on mortality tables, Petty had already made it clear that it was the duty of the government to ensure "peace and plenty" by increasing the number of goods available. His figures were instructions on how to act politically. *Political Arithmetick* described the effects of governance and pointed out where the government had to become active.

Petty was not interested in sober figures. For him, political goals were the primary driving force. A "very careless handling of figures" and "also a tendency to an imprecise account of the figures available" characterized his approach.[20] He often interpreted facts that the data available did not substantiate; he calculated missing figures by using dubious assumptions.

Although, by his own admission and firmly in the spirit of Bacon, Petty sought with his writings to improve the well-being of Crown and country, he was actually guided by the benefit it brought him personally. His statements on the possibility of taxing labor was intended to relieve his own class, the landowners, of further tax commitments. His political arithmetic was self-serving. The discovery of labor as a factor in taxation was not the result of research with an open outcome, but was derived from the intention of belittling the economic significance of his own class.[21]

The term "political arithmetic" was common in Europe for more than one hundred years. In the late eighteenth century, however, it was replaced by "statistics." Gottfried Achenwall, a philosopher and cameralist who taught in Göttingen, used the term for the first time in 1749 to describe the collection and evaluation of data of significance to the state. Statistics covered anything one had to know for the state, and about it.

Statistics, however, was merely the preparation and collection of data and information intended to give the state the broadest possible picture of the country's condition. This differed from Petty's approach in one important detail: Petty not only prepared or gathered data; he also combined it, thus giving it meaning. By combining data, he created a methodological framework of his own, with which he not only presented the economic situation but also, above all, interpreted it—and indeed thought he could predict it. In other words, he did not produce an image of reality; his method of presentation created a reality of its own. He developed a calculative practice that defined the parameters for economic and social processes and, as such, subsequently justified certain policies on the part of the public authorities. It also enabled the formulation of recommendations for future actions.[22]

In the two hundred years after Petty's death, no further attempt was made to calculate the income of a country—which later became known as the national income—as thoroughly and publicly as Petty had done, even though national income was repeatedly estimated in various countries.[23] Despite his innovative approach and his high standards, Petty was unable to use his political arithmetic to make any precise recommendations for government action. Even his contemporaries regarded his figures as insufficiently credible.

PETTY AND THE CONSEQUENCES: ADAM SMITH'S VIEW OF THE NATIONAL PRODUCT

Scottish moral philosopher Adam Smith, whose 1776 *Inquiry into the Nature and Causes of the Wealth of Nations* established economics as a science in its own right, was not convinced by political arithmetic. He makes no mention whatever of Petty in his epochal work, writing instead tersely: "I have no great faith in political arithmetic."[24]

Smith was not interested in combining current figures, even if his book relied on data to underpin his theories. He wanted primarily to develop a comprehensive, general theory of economic progress and to answer the question of how and why countries attain wealth. In doing so, he employed the idea of "annual produce," without elaborating on it methodically or going more precisely into the basis for the calculation—or even, as Petty had done, actually calculating the volume of this produce. His basic message was, however, unmistakable: the more goods produced in a country, the better.

For Smith, the ever more refined division of labor was the key to greater production. He saw no potential for this in agriculture. As a consequence, he logically assumed that, in the course of historical development, there was a gradual shift in the economic activities of a country, from agriculture to manufacturing, which inevitably led to increasing foreign trade. Everybody benefited from the rise in production and the division of labor: "It is the great multiplication of the productions of all the different arts, in consequence of the division of labour, which occasions, in a well-governed society, that universal opulence which extends itself to the lowest ranks of the people."[25]

For Smith, the fact that there was economic development and division of labor at all lay in the nature of humankind. He postulated a biological "desire of bettering our condition, a desire which, though generally calm and dispassionate, comes with us from the womb, and never leaves us till we go into the grave. In the whole interval which separates these two moments there is scarce perhaps a single instant in which any man is so perfectly and completely satisfied with his situation as to be without any wish of alteration or improvement of any kind."[26] The increase in their own material wealth provided most people with an opportunity to give in to this desire, though it could never be completely satisfied. The desire for improvement, for ever greater material wealth, was infinite.

Smith saw another characteristic of human nature in "the propensity to truck, barter, and exchange one thing for another." In his view, both the tendency to trade things and the wish for an improvement in one's own lot not only differentiated humans from animals but also enabled the requisite cooperation and networking, which only an economic system gave rise to in the first place. For Smith, the result of exchange, personal interest, and division of labor was "a general plenty." Though there would always be differences between rich and poor, the increase in production would lessen the existing differences in society, at least in a material respect: "The accommodation of an European prince does not always so much exceed that of an industrious and frugal peasant, as the accommodation of the latter exceeds that of an African king, the absolute master of the lives and liberty of ten thousand naked savages."[27]

Economic development was "natural progress," and the improvement in material living conditions through the production of ever more goods was the "natural" course of the history of humankind. In this context Smith spoke of "annual produce" as the revenue from the land and from labor.[28]

There were political reasons for Smith to use the word *natural*. His *Wealth of Nations* was not a study of economic activity devoid of political deliberations. It was an attack on mercantilism, the attempt by the state to steer the destiny of the economy and, in particular, to regulate production. Furthermore, the book was aimed at the physiocrats, who saw the well-being of a country in the expansion valuation of agriculture alone. It was, however, the founder of physiocracy, the physician François Quesnay, who, with his 1758 *Tableau Economique*, introduced a fundamental idea to economic discussion. Quesnay spoke not only of the circle that defined the relationship between economic players but also of "*produit net*," a net product that, following the deduction of subsistence costs, could be defined as the value of additional production.[29] For Quesnay, this net product was created only in the agricultural sector, and from there it spread to other areas—a point with which Smith, with his focus on the production of goods, emphatically disagreed.

Because material progress, according to Smith, was a result of human nature, any state intervention in "natural" economic processes hindered a rise in affluence. Were people allowed to live out their inclinations, it would benefit everyone. It was in this context that the idea of the "invisible hand" originated.[30] If the people themselves were allowed to decide where they invested their assets (inasmuch as they were rich enough to be able to make investments), they would automatically choose those activities that not only promised the greatest profit but also most promoted the material wealth of the nation.

In the same section of *The Wealth of Nations* where Smith talks of the mode of action of the invisible hand, the term "annual produce" appears again, and Smith equates this with "annual revenue." Given that every investment was made with an increase in productivity in mind, every investor played a role in raising the annual revenue—the invisible hand ensured that the annual production and, as such, the annual income of society rose. According to Smith's doctrine with regard to the labor theory of value, every commodity has its "natural price," which corresponds to the effort exerted in the production of the commodity and primarily comprises labor costs, paid to workers in the form of wages. Without further ado, Smith could thus assume that "the annual revenue of every society is always precisely equal to the exchangeable value of the whole annual produce of its industry, or rather is precisely the same thing with that exchangeable value."[31] As with Petty's method, this insight was based on the principle of double bookkeeping, though Smith focused more on production and not, like Petty, on consumption.

Although Smith claimed that the state should not be directly involved in economic affairs, his ideas did give rise to a doctrine for the state. Political economics was a political science. For Smith, it was the state's duty to support natural development processes by improving overall conditions, organizing judicial and defense systems, and ensuring a just tax system. Political economics was meant to demonstrate how higher income could be achieved and thus the population's means of subsistence improved. At the same time, the state had to ensure that it had sufficient income to perform its duties. This is what Smith saw as a "well-governed society." As with Petty, Smith was of the opinion that the state had to ensure "peace and plenty" by putting in place the conditions for increasing the annual produce. As opposed to Petty, however, it was precisely *not* the interpretation of the relevant concrete annual produce figures that prompted Smith to make the conclusions he did. For him, his theoretical deliberations were decisive.

In Smith's view of the world, every individual had a place assigned to him or her by God. The social differences in a society were part of a divine order; rebelling against this was pointless. Smith regarded the inequality of rich and poor as natural; for him, the effect of the invisible hand was in evidence here: it was only the social differences that enabled everyone to live, because, by consuming, the wealthy ensured the livelihood of the poor. Rising material wealth was suitable for avoiding resentment and securing the social status quo.[32]

MALTHUS AND MARSHALL

In 1805, Thomas Robert Malthus, who had risen to fame in the late eighteenth century with his "Essay on the Principle of Population," according to which the production of foodstuffs in the world could not keep pace with the growth in population, which would inevitably and repeatedly lead to famine and suffering, became England's first professor of political economy. Malthus was convinced that only Adam Smith's book was as significant as his own *Principles of Political Economy*, a textbook on economic theory, which he published in 1820. Published posthumously, in 1836, the second edition contained several important methodic deliberations on national income.[33] Malthus did not calculate figures for the national income, but he did try to explain what had to be taken into consideration in any such undertaking. Nor did he use any one term for it, referring to "national income," "national wealth," "national revenue," and "national produce."

As Adam Smith had, Malthus, in the calculation of a country's wealth, restricted himself to the volume of material goods produced. According to Malthus, the reason for this was that, as opposed to the value of services and other immaterial goods, the value of material goods could be determined exactly: their value corresponded to the price they attained on the market. Furthermore, only material goods could be accumulated. Because he based his theories on their measurability, Malthus limited the parameters for the goods that contributed to a country's wealth. Anything not traded on the market was not included in the calculation.

Alfred Marshall described the idea of national income in detail in his epochal 1890 work *Principles of Economics*. For Marshall, too, only goods and services that could be evaluated monetarily should be included in the calculation of national income.[34] Unlike Malthus, however, Marshall factored in immaterial goods and services, provided they had a market price. With the help of the capital and labor in a country, a certain amount of these goods and services were produced annually. A country's annual net income could be determined by including the income from investments abroad, and by deducting the capital spent on the production process from the value of the goods or services produced. Given that everything produced was intended for consumption, the value of consumption aggregates would correspond to those of production. Consumption was negative production.[35]

For Marshall, like Smith before him, economics was the science of wealth. Wealth was created through goods, and goods were basically all those things with which people could satisfy their needs, and could be measured in monetary units.[36] For Marshall, however, increasing the amount of goods was a greater social policy necessity than for Smith. Economics was meant to help solve the social question—to alleviate the mass impoverishment that had resulted from industrialization. Improving material living conditions by increasing the national income was a prerequisite for fighting poverty. For Smith, an increased "annual produce" also automatically promised the lower classes, across the board, a better material life. In Marshall's time, however, fighting poverty had become the most urgent domestic problem, particularly because, since 1834, the "New Poor Law" had marked the end of the state subsidies for the poor that had been introduced in 1597.

PIGOU AND WELFARE

It was British economist Arthur Cecil Pigou, Marshall's successor to his chair at Cambridge, who explored the topic in greater detail. The question of national income plays an outstanding role in his 1920 work *The Economics of Welfare.* The entire book, the fourth edition of which is almost nine hundred pages long, addresses the question of the influence the national income exerts on various areas of the national economy and on a country's total welfare.[37]

Like Marshall, Pigou deliberated on the basic function of economics, as well as on how it could be differentiated from other sciences. What was so special about it? What made it more important than other disciplines? For Pigou, who agreed with Marshall on this, the function of economics as a science was to improve the social situation. The main feature of economics had to be the identification of practical measures to increase welfare, the term Pigou used instead of "wealth."

"Welfare," however, covered a broad spectrum. Even though Pigou failed to state precisely what he meant by the term, he was sure that welfare could be divided into the categories "less" or "more," and that although several aspects could be measured empirically, others could not. For Pigou, the most obvious instrument of measurement in social life was money. For this reason, he too restricted himself to "that part of social welfare that can be brought directly or indirectly into relation with the measuring-rod of money."[38]

Pigou called that part of welfare measurable in money "economic welfare." This formed part of general or social welfare. It was not possible to draw an exact line between the scientific and the nonscientific components that made up welfare. Concentrating on money, however, allowed a sufficient restriction of the area of economic investigation. Though there could be no certainty that total welfare rose as soon as there was a rise in economic welfare, according to Pigou, it was highly probable that changes in the latter at least had a positive impact on total welfare.[39]

Given that it was not economic activities that directly increased welfare, but rather the generation and use of national income, Pigou saw a link between it and economic welfare. For this reason, economic welfare could only be measured with the measuring rod of money in the form of national income.[40] And if national economy rose, one could assume, until the contrary was proved, that total welfare rose as well.

Pigou was well aware of the paradoxes with regard to the method of measuring national income: "If a man marries his housekeeper or his cook, the national dividend is diminished," he commented prosaically.[41]

The idea of national income was a feature of economics from the outset, and was methodically refined over the years. It was, however, a factor that was considered merely theoretical, with no concrete political significance; calculating the national income and making it the basis for political decisions was not deemed necessary. For this reason, and not just because there was a lack of relevant data, governments did not determine their national incomes. No one, not even economists, believed in the necessity of political arithmetic in the style of Petty until well into the twentieth century. Many economists even considered the idea that increasing production could contribute to wealth or welfare, and thus help resolve the social question, to be methodically irrelevant. Expanding production was just as little the aim of direct political planning. As late as 1932, for example, the British economist Lionel Robbins published an "Essay on the Nature and Significance of Economic Science," in which he interpreted the role of economics as a science: economists should investigate and model human behavior with a view to deciding among scarce goods. Robbins rejected as unscientific the view that economists should investigate the reasons for material wealth. Possible political and sociopolitical impacts on social life were beyond the boundaries of economic science. A term such as "wealth" had no place in economic theory: "We cannot define wealth in physical terms as we can define food in terms of vitamin content or calorific value. It is an essentially relative concept."[42] In his opinion, something similar applied to national income.

3

THE FRUSTRATIONS OF COLIN CLARK

England

Colin Clark (1905–1989) was one of the most important modern pioneers of gross domestic product. He formulated many of what are still today standard elements in the compilation of GDP, made his own calculations of national income, and linked these calculations to two ideas that were previously totally unknown: the concept of growth and the growth rate of the national income as a measure of economic progress, and the idea of using national income as a key performance indicator for international comparisons. Clark's deliberations would have a revolutionary effect: that changed what we understand as "progress" and, above all, changed forever how we see the world. Both of these aspects were crucial for the later political triumph of GDP.

Clark also has been recognized as one of the most important pioneers of development theory. His works on the calculation of the national economy were foundational to the concept of economic development and underdevelopment, which involves the measurement of development by per capita income.[1]

William Petty was Clark's great role model, and Clark wanted to adapt Petty's idea of a political arithmetic to the requirements of the new era. Although Clark's works on national income were not kept under lock and key, as Petty's had been, he by no means enjoyed the support one would expect, given the ultimate importance of his work for the present-day calculation of GDP. His ideas and measurements succeeded neither in academia nor in politics. All his life, Clark expressed his bitterness about his lack of scholarly success and political influence.

NATIONAL INCOME (AND CONTRACEPTION)

Colin Clark's father, James, came from Scotland and immigrated to Australia in 1878. He amassed his fortune exporting wool and meat, and in 1905 returned to Great Britain, where his son Colin was born shortly after. After several years in London, the family moved to a farm near Plymouth, England.[2]

Clark studied chemistry at Oxford, at the same college at which William Petty had taught, and he initially stayed on at the university as a chemist, after graduation. Out of interest and curiosity, he regularly attended events hosted by a group of economists, who addressed questions of economic policy. As a natural scientist, he was put off by the way the experts discussed economic matters. The economic science he encountered seemed too theoretical, too deductive, insufficiently empirical, and unsuited to the topic of investigation. Having studied Petty's writings closely, Clark devoted his free time to collecting and preparing economic data himself. Petty's opinion that only data and empiricism can create knowledge, and that state activity should be based on an analysis of the figures available, corresponded with Clark's ideal of how economists should work.

Clark impressed not only the members of the discussion group but also leading economists at Oxford with his empirically substantiated explanations of the dire economic situation. They encouraged him to intensify his studies and managed to secure him an appointment as a research assistant for some of the most eminent empirical researchers of the day. For instance, he collaborated with William Beveridge, the pioneer of the welfare state in Britain, on studies of the socioeconomic situation in London and Liverpool.

In 1930, Clark was appointed as a research assistant to the National Economic Advisory Council, which had recently been created by the Labour government. This was the first time that a committee of experts would advise the British government on economic policy. The government was at a loss as to how to cope with the worsening global economic crisis of the Great Depression, especially because no one knew what was actually happening; although the social effects of the crisis were obvious, there were no exact numbers to describe the phenomenon.

The illustrious members of this group included John Maynard Keynes and Arthur Pigou, who were already world-famous economists. The politicians, however, proved to be impervious to advice, and despite all the arguments put forward by the council, they continued to pursue standard economic ideas such as protectionism. "In that government,"

Clark later said, looking back on his experience in the advisory body, "the Prime Minister ought to have been in a mental hospital, the chancellor of the Exchequer was physically incapacitated, and the Minister in charge of economic policy was a crook."[3] The discussions in the council were often "confused and senseless." Nevertheless, Clark was able to present some of his statistical works and interpretations to the council, making a lasting impression on Keynes and Pigou, even though he had only just turned twenty-five and had no formal education in economics. In an age in which people craved new information and data, Clark quickly gained a reputation as a statistical prodigy.[4]

After resigning, disappointed, from the council, Clark ran on several occasions for Parliament for the Labour Party, but failed miserably. Pigou and Keynes, who were both teaching at Cambridge, secured him a position as lecturer in statistics. It was neither well paid nor particularly prestigious, but Clark remained at Cambridge from 1931 to 1937. He was in the right place at the right time, as these were the years in which Keynes was working on his epochal book *The General Theory of Employment, Interest, and Money* (1936) and was on the point of revolutionizing economics. Clark provided Keynes with statistical data that no one else was capable of generating. As early as 1932, in his book *The National Income, 1924–1931*, Clark presented a consistent estimation of the development of national income in Britain and made pioneering methodological observations on the recording and definition of the national income.[5] Though Keynes thought highly of the work, he only quoted it once in his *General Theory*.

Clark became increasingly dissatisfied with his situation. He was not moving up the academic hierarchy at the university, politicians paid no attention to his ideas about calculating the national income along the lines of a modern, Petty-style political arithmetic, and it seemed he would not fulfill his own political ambitions. So, in 1937, he took leave of his position at the university and, like his father, sought his fortune in Australia. There he intended to move forward with his works on national income while also gaining a foothold in politics. Shortly before leaving England, he published his second book about the theory of the calculation, *National Income and Outlay*, in which he further refined his methodological deliberations.[6]

Australia offered Clark optimal conditions. He was fascinated by the socioeconomic circumstances in Queensland, where he was able to pursue both politics and science. With just over one million inhabitants and a surface area of almost two million hectares, blessed with mineral resources, the state seemed like a paradise in comparison with Great Britain. The differences in income were small, the trade unions were strong, legislation was employee friendly, and unlike in England, there was already a functioning social security system. When Clark was offered the vacant position of financial adviser to Queensland Territory, in 1938, he resigned from his position at Cambridge. Two years later, his most important book appeared: *The Conditions of Economic Progress*.[7]

Australia was regarded as methodologically advanced in the field of national income statistics. Almost unnoticed by the rest of the world, an engineer named Timothy Coghlan had estimated income in the province of New South Wales in the late nineteenth century.[8] For the first time in the history of the calculation of national income, this estimate was published in an official statistical yearbook. By the turn of the century, these income statistics had been extended to all of Australia's states, but they were scrapped in 1904 due to a lack of long-term political interest in the figures.[9]

Another of Australia's peculiarities was the influence of Catholicism on politics there. Catholics played a decisive role in both the Labor Party and the government. Colin Clark converted to Catholicism; for him, economics was not independent of moral considerations. He advocated early marriage, lots of children, and agricultural self-sufficiency. Clark saw the ideal society as cooperative and decentralized. People should live in the country, he thought, not in inhuman big cities and metropolises.[10] Clark himself set an example of such a life: he acquired a country estate near Brisbane, farmed it, kept cows and pigs, and—fulfilling the biblical requirement of reproduction—fathered eight sons.[11]

In his later years, Clark argued vehemently against the neo-Malthusian school of thought. In the 1960s, overpopulation was considered to be one of the main threats to human survival, with Garrett Hardin's influential 1968 article "The Tragedy of the Commons" conjuring up a horror scenario of overpopulation, as predicted by Malthus one hundred fifty years before. In Clark's view, however, a growing global population would not endanger humanity, because of the potential growth in gross national product (GNP, which by then had supplanted the concept of national income). As long as economic growth continued—and Clark had no doubt that this would be possible for a very, very long time—a growing global population could also be fed. Clark made his position clear in his best-known book, *Population Growth and Land Use*, published in 1967.[12]

Clark's theories found an appreciative audience in certain circles. In 1964, Pope Paul VI appointed him an economic adviser in the Vatican Commission on Birth Control. This commission advised the Holy See on the formulation of the encyclical *Humanae Vitae*, which forbade Catholics to use contraception. Clark played a major role in justifying the ban on contraception, not on theological but on economic grounds. As an economist he considered contraception unnecessary, and as a Catholic he rejected it for reasons of faith. Without his works on national income and gross national product, Clark would probably never have become the voice of economic reason on the papal commission.

Colin Clark was one of the last classical political economists. As with the pioneers of political arithmetic, his aim was to provide the state with sensible, data-based decision-making tools. At the same time, however, he had a clear moral conception of what made for a good community. He was often accused of letting his conversion to Catholicism exert too great an influence on his academic works. Clark's reply was that it was not that Catholicism had influenced him, but that, in Catholicism, he had discovered morals that concurred with his convictions. But it was probably less his extreme shift to Catholicism than his leaving England that excluded Clark from further methodological discussions about national income.

CLARK'S WRITINGS ON NATIONAL INCOME

When Clark set out to revolutionize the method of calculating national income, with his 1932 book *The National Income, 1924–1931*, the last estimate was quite old: no calculation of the national income had been conducted in Great Britain since 1924. However, because the estimate had been made using an income approach, and showed the income differences among various social classes, the employers' associations had prevented its publication, out of fear that the figures could prompt the trade unions to demand wage increases.[13] For Clark, this kind of censorship was scandalous.

From his experience as a government official, Clark knew that politicians still lacked suitable data with which to explain the economic situation. He wanted not only to provide these figures but also to demonstrate how useful regular calculation of the national income would be. Clark was not commissioned to write the book; he published it on his own account.

Never before had Great Britain seen a book about national income that was so detailed and brimming with data and tables. Indeed, no other economic publication was so entirely based on empiricism as Clark's book. It contained page-long explanations of how he had gleaned the information he needed from existing data, and which suppositions he had had to make to get the desired figures.

Clark had the very latest production and tax estimates available, which he used to derive his data. However, he was unimpressed with the quality of British statistics. His great achievement was to tirelessly gather figures from all manner of sources, or to calculate them himself; his book was the result of years of sometimes frenzied, manic searching for data, which had begun early on, during the time he spent in Oxford. Trying to complete his calculations was, he said, like trying to make clay bricks without straw. He vehemently, but unsuccessfully, pleaded for economic data to be recorded centrally—and regularly—by state authorities.

In keeping with Marshall, Clark defined national income as the sum total of the market price of all goods and services, which, taking intermediate consumption into consideration, is available for consumption in a specific period. Because this figure included depreciation (i.e., consumption of fixed capital), national income was a "gross" income measure.[14] This is why Clark is regarded as the inventor of the modern concept of gross national product, without having used this specific term himself.

In his book, Clark implemented a decisive new method. He calculated national income using what are today the three standard approaches: from the production side, the income side, and the expenditure side. His three results did not exactly match each other, but Clark had not expected them to do so, given the uncertainty of the data available. Still, he wanted to show that a calculation of national income from three different angles could make the overall measure more plausible and more credible. Should the results at least match in terms of general magnitude, the general information about national income would be understood to be less arbitrary than previously assumed.[15]

Clark's achieved his calculation of national income on the income side, relying on tax data and wage statistics. The data available for production and expenditure, however, was insufficient for a precise calculation of national income.[16] As such, the measure remained a calculation of income, both methodologically and in name; the level of production could only be estimated. From the data for 1924, Clark then extrapolated the trends until 1931.

Another innovation came in the last chapter of Clark's book, where he used his results to illustrate how certain aggregate macroeconomic parameters had changed from 1924 to 1931. He showed that it was possible, from the data, to gain an idea of how consumption, savings patterns, the size of the active population, and other indictors developed. There previously had been no informative calculations of these.

Clark's approach was pioneering for the further development of economic statistics. By combining figures, he showed, in the words of British historian Alexander Cairncross, "how to *play* with statistics: how, by means of a little speculative arithmetic, to mix statistics that were firm with statistics that were far from firm and arrive at conclusions of major importance in resolving issues of economic policy.... At the same time he helped to revolutionize governmental use of statistics for current policy by encouraging the *estimation* of economic aggregates."[17]

Clark was the only British researcher to make estimates of national income in the 1930s. In the foreword to *National Income and Outlay* (1937), he complained, already clearly embittered, about the lack of financial and personal support. If economics were to improve humankind's lot, the resources available for research had to be increased, particularly for data collection and analysis, not for theoretical speculation.[18]

The very word *outlay* in the title of his new book indicated that Clark was no longer merely concerned with measuring income but also with what people spent. In addition to new calculations of national income, *National Income and Outlay* also attempted to estimate the trend in national income since the early nineteenth century. Clark was original in giving quarterly calculations of national income, taking seasonal fluctuations into account. He also presented his own measurement of progress: the rate of change in per capita income of the active population. In the previous eighty years, there had been greater economic progress in Great Britain than in the four hundred before. By calculating per capita income, it was possible to substantiate the exact rate of change and to identify the phases when, because of adverse economic conditions, there had been a fall in income. Furthermore, the data he prepared showed that, even where capital accumulation and investment volume dropped, there were rises in productivity and thus in incomes. This contradicted the common view that the accumulation of capital was the source of economic growth and progress.

In the 1939 book *A Critique of Russian Statistics*, Clark explored the method behind and the quality of Soviet statistics, which in the early twentieth century were regarded as particularly highly developed. He recalculated the Soviet national income by using his own method, basing the evaluation of individual goods on English prices; since Soviet prices were regulated by the state, Clark did not think they allowed for informative analysis.[19]

In this book, Clark provided a simple definition of national income based on production: "The only valid and complete measure of economic progress is the figure of National Income—by definition the value of goods and services produced during the year, available for consumption, or investment."[20] According to Clark, only this figure could provide an exact picture of the entire economy.

THE CONDITIONS OF ECONOMIC PROGRESS

Clark's 1940 work *The Conditions of Economic Progress* is undoubtedly his most important. Basing his work on Smith's *Wealth of Nations*, Clark wanted to determine the conditions that needed to be fulfilled for a country "to be able to hope for the highest degree of economic progress."[21] He did so by collecting, evaluating, and comparing all national income data available worldwide. It was a monumental task. "In an era of slide rules and adding machines," as British economic historian Angus Maddison put it, Clark spent four years working on it.[22]

Again affirming his affinity to the ideas of Petty, Clark featured one of Francis Bacon's dictums in his book: "It cannot be that axioms established by argumentation can suffice for the discovery of new works, for the subtilty of Nature exceedeth many times over the subtilty of argument."[23]

Clark was still very dissatisfied with economists. Not even one in a hundred knew what scientific work was, he complained. Science was based on the systematization of all observable facts, from which hypotheses could then be derived, which then had to be corroborated by facts in turn. The way economists theorized would have been "laughable," said Clark, "were it not tragic."[24] With William Petty, economics had become a science, but since Smith, it had gone off in the wrong direction. It was obvious to Clark how this had to be corrected—by a return to the inventor of political arithmetic.[25] Only that would serve humanity. "There is room for two or three economic theorists in each generation, not more. Only men of transcendental powers of reasoning can be candidates for these positions. . . . The rest of us should be economic scientists, content steadily to lay stone on stone in building the structure of ordered knowledge."[26]

For Clark, economics had a clear position in the hierarchy of sciences. Although it was dominant over certain disciplines, he maintained, economists had to be aware that their subject was subordinate to political science. Only the relevant political system generated a common good.[27] Petty's idea of political arithmetic also was based on the fundamental concept that politics was the field toward which economics had to work.

According to Clark, the economy was exclusively about things that could be bought and sold. Economic progress— a higher national income—meant an improvement in economic welfare, à la Pigou. But clearly this measure could not cover all possible aspects of welfare and well-being, and especially not those things that made life valuable.[28] Although calculating and comparing national income was certainly useful in itself, national economic statistics would only help generate knowledge if they were compared with results from other countries. This was the reasoning behind Clark's international comparisons of national incomes, something that was extremely unusual for his time.[29]

To compare national income data worldwide, Clark used an innovative trick. He constructed a currency unit, the "international unit," which was based on the theory of purchasing power parity and was the precursor of today's purchasing power parity exchange rates. Clark defined the value of an international unit as "the amount of goods and services which one dollar would purchase in the USA over the average of the period 1925–1934."[30]

In his comparison of countries by their national income data, Clark arrived at an alarming result. Expressed in figures, the discrepancy was far more dramatic than supposed: "The world is found to be a wretchedly poor place." Four countries—the United States, Great Britain, France, and Germany, which accounted for 13 percent of the world's population—produced almost half of worldwide income. The United States and Canada were fourteen times as rich as the poorest parts of the world. "The age of plenty will still be a long while in coming," Clark concluded.[31]

The differences in affluence around the world were "astonishing" to Clark—hardly anyone had reckoned on such immense differences in global wealth. According to Clark, countries considered to be extremely poor were those with a per capita income of less than two hundred international units per year for the working (active) population; in the United States, the figure was 1,400 international units. More than half the world's population suffered poverty of this kind.[32] In large parts of the globe, survival seemed scarcely possible. Only a few years later, development aid was viewed as indispensable—and this opinion was largely due to the dramatic picture that Clark's figures painted.[33]

Furthermore, Clark's analyses demonstrated that, in the course of its economic development, a country's employment structure shifted from the agricultural and production sectors to the service sector. The share of a particular sector in the national income was thus indicative in each case of a country's stage of development. Clark called the dynamics of this three-sector model Petty's law, because Petty, in his political arithmetic, had suggested a similar pattern of development.

According to this logic, a rise in per capita income was possible when the working population shifted from the primary sector to the two other sectors. This made a Malthusian scenario of enduring poverty, in which many people had to eke out a living on the minimum subsistence level, less and less likely. For Clark, the biggest challenge the world faced was to increase production capacities. He saw the hallmark of economic progress in the shift to more and more production in the secondary and tertiary sectors, and in the expanded production of goods and services. Economic growth of this nature would pave road to prosperity, which promised an end to poverty—just as classical economists in the past had argued, albeit on the basis of theoretical deliberations.

Despite its methodological innovations and findings, Clark did not achieve much glory with this book, either. This was thanks in part to the bewildering wealth of statistical data, presented over more than seven hundred pages. He often let the figures speak for themselves, so much so that he was accused of not supporting his statements with a consistent theory, or of not having a theory of his own at all. According to his critics, Clark all too often confused the quantity of the data with their quality.[34] In this context, Angus Maddison wrote:

> Colin Clark was a loner, bubbling with ideas and handling a vast amount of material in *Conditions of Economic Progress*. He presented the reader with a mass of primary material, whose analytical relevance was frequently difficult to perceive. He had hundreds of tables, but in the first two editions, none of them was numbered, many had no title and countries were not listed in alphabetical order. . . . His bibliographical references were frequently inadequate, often omitting dates or titles. This was not true of his work in the 1930s on national income. . . . The disorderly presentation of his *magnum opus* and the difficulty in digesting it is a major reason why his distinguished role in the history of macro-measurement is often underestimated. . . . If he had concentrated his efforts and been less impatient to cover so many problems, his impact would probably have been greater.[35]

THE INFLUENCE ON BRITISH POLITICS OF CALCULATING NATIONAL INCOME

Until 1940, there were few international surveys of statistically aggregated parameters. Statistics, including economic statistics, were available but were neither linked to nor coordinated with one another and were for the most part gathered unsystematically.[36]

Despite Clark's publications, the British government did not initially commission the calculation of national income or take it into consideration in governmental decision-making processes. Clark remained, as economist Don Patinkin put it, "a voice crying in the wilderness."[37] This was due in part to his departure from the British Isles, but also to the British economists' traditional lack of interest in empirical research. Although Keynes recognized great potential in Clark's studies, for example, he was extremely critical of the quality of these statistical presentations, and until war broke out, he did nothing to convince the government of the sense and necessity of a statistical coverage of national income. In his *General Theory* (1936), Keynes had still spoken of the calculation of national income as serving only to satisfy "historical curiosity."[38] The idea that calculations of this nature could be politically or analytically meaningful was still remote to him.

Lionel Robbins also found the pure summation of prices or individual incomes to calculate a specific figure as national income to be meaningless. This aggregate, he said, was only of "conventional significance."[39] He maintained that it did not reflect any facts of reality but had only come about on account of its own definition of itself and through arbitrary suppositions. Though collecting statistics of this nature was not meaningless, one had to be clear about the conventions they were based on and must not mistake the values calculated with reality.

Keynes's critical stance changed suddenly with the outbreak of the World War II and the need for continuous, up-to-date data about the state of the economy. The war was the "birth of National Accounts" and ushered in a "statistical revolution."[40] When war broke out, Keynes considered it imperative that the government be given a basis of calculation to understand the means available for war spending. This required the estimation of a realistic tax basis, and an answer to the question of how much money could be generated through taxes. His financing plan, which he presented in 1940 in a book entitled *How to Pay for the War*, was based on higher taxation and compulsory saving. The war should be financed not through voluntary payments (such as war bonds), he said, but by freezing social services and imposing higher taxes. It was also crucial to avoid inflation.

Keynes wanted to know how much of the cake would be left for civil consumption after the spending on the war had been deducted.[41] To that end, he had to estimate the potential industrial output that could be realized if all available resources were used. That meant that the state—as was characteristic of Keynes's revolutionary theories—had to be given a central role. In this, Keynes departed fundamentally from the position Colin Clark had adopted in his calculations. In the logic behind Clark's calculation of national income, there was no focus on the state's spending, which for Clark was not a final product but intermediate consumption that would not be counted. For Keynes, on the other hand, government spending was an important economic policy instrument in times of crisis. For this reason, he proposed another definition of national income in *How to Pay for the War*: in addition to private consumption and investment, government expenditure spending should also be included. Keynes called the resulting figure "taxable income."[42]

The second book of the *General Theory* already contained a definition and combination of certain macroeconomic aggregates. It read:

Income = Value of output = Consumption + Investment.
Saving = Income – Consumption.
Therefore, Saving = Investment.[43]

Keynes was aware that a coherent and coordinated system of accounts, in which important economic aggregates were recorded, could empirically underpin his theoretical deliberations and help establish as standard his interpretation of the way the economy functioned. Adjusting how national income was calculated, such that it supported his theory, was doubtless a matter of concern to him.

On the basis of his own ideas, Keynes, together with Erwin Rothbarth, compiled estimates of the national economy. Rothbarth, a trusted colleague who totally agreed with Keynes on the recalibration of national income, hailed from Germany, had studied economic science at the London School of Economics, and worked as Keynes's research assistant at Cambridge. After a brief internment in the summer of 1940, he enlisted voluntarily with the British army. He was killed in action in 1944.[44]

As early as 1939, Keynes and Rothbarth published an article in the *Economic Journal*, in which they critically addressed Clark's method of calculation and explained why economic policy should focus on income that was relevant for tax purposes, not on income available to the private sector. Because this income was generated from the production of goods and services, government spending had to be included.[45] Furthermore, Clark's calculations did not seem sufficiently expedient. The statistics Clark had used, they maintained, were inadequate: "There is no one to-day, inside or outside government offices, who does not mainly depend on the brilliant private efforts of Mr. Colin Clark. . . . But in the absence of statistics . . . he could often do no better than make a brave guess."[46] With his methodological adjustments, Keynes believed he had overcome Clark's inadequacies.

Of course, the British government still had to wake up to the significance of such calculations. "Every government since the last war has been unscientific and obscurantist, and has regarded the collection of essential facts as a waste of money," Keynes wrote in *How to Pay for the War*.[47] Along with him, it was primarily the economist Austin Robinson—an adviser to the War Cabinet, later a professor at Cambridge, and, like Keynes, an editor of the *Economic Journal*—who ensured that this changed. After reading *How to Pay for the War*, Robinson pushed the War Cabinet to commission an estimate of national income, using the new Keynesian method, so as to plan the war activities. The Treasury appointed two employees to the task: James Meade and Richard Stone.[48]

Stone (1913–1991) had been one of Clark's pupils and, after Clark left England, he advanced his teacher's method of calculation. Meade (1907–1995) had already worked on international income statistics at the League of Nations (although these were merely informative in character). Meade was extremely familiar with Keynesian theory, whereas Stone was initially very much influenced by Clark's ideas. Stone, however, was one of the few who knew Simon Kuznets's writings and the American discussion of the method of national income accounting (to be discussed further in the next chapter). At the Treasury, Meade's and Stone's offices were only a few steps away from Keynes's, who at the time was also working as an adviser there. Keynes monitored their work closely and together they agreed on every step.[49]

It was Meade and Stone who systematized Clark's ideas and concepts and who ensured that an internationally valid methodological framework for national accounts was established in the long term, in the System of National Accounts (SNA). (In recognition of his contribution, Stone was risen to the peerage in 1978 and was awarded the Nobel Prize in Economics in 1984.) Keynes, however, was actively involved in establishing a method of national income accounting that reflected the inner logic of short-term economic trends depicted in his *General Theory*, and he subsequently ensured that his pupils were placed in important political interfaces.

Because Keynes died in 1946, and Meade's and Stone's accounts system only became generally established in the following years, Keynes's direct personal influence on the definition of national income and its method of calculation is often underestimated, even though the national accounts system is perhaps his greatest and most enduring success.

In April 1941, just in time for the government's budget negotiations, Meade and Stone presented a white paper entitled "Analysis of the Sources of War Finance and Estimate of the National Income and Expenditure in 1938 and 1940." As had been the case with Clark and Petty, the figures were the result of combinations rather than mere compilations of economic transactions, and contained estimates. Some of the figures could only be determined as residuals. Given the uncertainty involved, the official publication of the calculations was politically risky and historically unique for a government body. It was thanks to Keynes's pressure and influence that the government skepticism was not overwhelming.

It was this white paper that marked the transition from the simple statistical recording of national income to related, interdependent national accounts.[50] Clark had laid the foundation for this, but he lacked a consistent system of accounts that included his individual fields of investigation. Meade and Stone delivered this accounts system, though it was based on Keynes's and Rothbarth's definition.

The meshing of various accounts became the main methodological approach for national accounting. The system was intended to be structured so that the most important information was visible, while at the same time a "maximum amount of statistical cross-checking" was possible.[51] By cross-referencing, the calculated aggregates could be checked for different data recording levels and accounts. Meade and Stone kept the triple method of calculation introduced by Clark: income distribution, production, and expenditure were recorded separately, and the results were to be numerically identical. For Meade and Stone, the idea that the three numbers calculated by the three different approaches were identical was an important assumption, an a priori definition.

Meade and Stone presented their approach in an article in the *Economic Journal*, which appeared soon after the white paper. With the very title, "The Construction of Tables of

National Income, Expenditure, Savings, and Investment," the authors made quite clear what their system of accounts had made possible: methodologically consistent, comprehensible, and plausible calculations of aggregated values such as national income, expenditure, saving, and investment.

The application of factor costs represented an important difference from the American method of recording the national economy, which was being developed at the same time. Factor costs are determined by deducting indirect taxes from the market price and by adding subsidies. This figure corresponds to the income of the factors of production (for example, labor, in the form of wages).[52] When focusing on factor costs, reflections on productivity play a greater role.[53] According to Keynes, applying the factor costs provided a more exact picture of the economic situation; market prices, on the other hand, tended to be distracting. Furthermore, in contrast to earlier theories, Keynesian theory focused primarily on the factors that determine demand on product markets. Taking the factor costs into consideration underscored this focus on demand.

Meade's and Stone's system spoke to two different aspirations: for a more accurate, more easily comprehensible depiction of economic processes and contexts, and for a method of calculation that should, through universal acceptance, make an international comparison of the aggregated values possible.[54] They were well aware of the extraordinary nature of their work. Not only were they politically enshrining a certain method of calculation but also, parallel to this, they were positively sanctioning a certain way of interpreting economic processes. After the appearance of the white paper,

Stone wrote, "It was a great day. We drank champagne that night and felt we accomplished something."[55]

Upon publication of the paper, responsibility for calculating national income passed to the newly established Central Statistical Office, of which Richard Stone became head. Here, too, Keynes had a hand in things, insisting that Stone be awarded the position.[56]

Only now could one create an exact picture of the interaction among aspects of the economy in Great Britain. As long as there was a lack of relevant data, it was scarcely possible to plan war production. Now, quarterly bulletins were produced, in which one could see the situation of the working population, whether the expansion of the armaments industry had led to bottlenecks in other important areas of the economy, and what stock levels were doing. (Previously, not even those in the planning units involved with aircraft production, for example, knew how many propellers were being produced.)[57] The government was suddenly able to paint an overall picture of economic processes.

Through Keynes's ideas, the recording of national income was given a theoretical basis it had previously lacked. Previously, national income was the result of empirical research, explicitly forgoing a theoretical superstructure.[58] With the adoption of Keynesian ideas, national income became a key measure, as did the associated economic aggregates, which Keynes saw as particularly important. This referred especially to investment—a key factor in the calculation of national income, key to the generation of income itself, and an important state policy option in the form of government spending.

Meade's and Stone's national accounts were political arithmetic in the best sense of Clark and Petty. This system did not, however, accord national income itself, or its growth rate, any all-deciding importance. There was no single figure to which all elements had been related. Rather, the system of accounts gave rise to an overall impression of the economy, even if it were expressed and summarized in just a few aggregates. The political focus was more on the income generated (i.e., the tax basis) and less on production. No one single powerful figure emerged from the logic of this system—but in America, things turned out differently.

4

SIMON KUZNETS AND THE POLITICS OF GROSS NATIONAL PRODUCT

The United States

In the case of the United States, it was Congress—and thus the state in the widest sense—that first sensed how useful statistics on the calculation of national income could be. Simon Kuznets (1901–1985) played an outstanding role in this, but although his work accelerated the advance of political arithmetic, he fell out with the state institutions responsible for calculating the figures for national income. Nonetheless, his failure ensured that the concept of gross national product emerged as a political constant in America. Kuznets no longer had any political support for his ideas, but others used his ideas for their own purposes—leading ultimately to a shift in focus from national income to gross national product.

In 1971, Kuznets was awarded the Nobel Prize for Economics, though not for his work on national income, like Richard Stone, but specifically for his research into the phenomenon of economic growth. Kuznets distinguished himself with his research into inequality; in his most famous article, "Economic Growth and Income Inequality" (1955), he investigated how income inequality developed during times of economic growth.[1] On the basis of historical data from England, the United States, and Germany, he demonstrated that, as the pace of growth picked up, income inequality first increased, before later falling again. Kuznets examined whether this phenomenon could also be discerned in developing countries that, since the 1950s, had channeled all their economic efforts into achieving higher growth. The linkage Kuznets uncovered was ideally suited for graphic representation: it came to be called the Kuznets curve and has become an iron law in economics, with researchers repeatedly testing its validity.[2]

Reliance on empirical evidence was characteristic of Kuznets's approach. It's not without reason that he was described as "exemplar economic empiricist of the century."[3] As was the case for Colin Clark, the collection and precise analysis of figures had priority for Kuznets. Only on this basis was it possible to identify and describe the theoretical foundations of what was under observation.

EMPIRICISM AND CAUTION

Simon Kuznets was born in 1901 in Pinsk, in czarist Russia. He was the son of a furrier. During World War I, the family fled to Kharkiv, in Ukraine, where Kuznets attended high school and later university, to study economics. At the time, Russian statistics were seen as the most advanced in the world, and Russian economics had a far more empirical focus than elsewhere. Following the closure of the University of Kharkiv during the Russian Civil War, the Bolsheviks tasked Kuznets with heading a department in the Bureau of Labor Statistics. Soon afterwards, the Kuznets family immigrated to America, where Simon studied at Columbia University in New York.

Empirical social research was flourishing in the United States as a result of the ever-growing optimism that the social sciences could have a true *scientific* footing, and that this would help lead to solutions to the pressing political and social problems of the day. More and more philanthropic foundations were financing empirical research. As early as 1916, Robert S. Brookings founded the Institute for Government Research, which in 1927 became the Brookings Institution. In 1920, the National Bureau of Economic Research (NBER) was established in New York, and in 1923, the Social Science Research Council was formed.[4] The intention of these foundations was to promote research that was independent of ideological presuppositions. Kuznets began work at the NBER in 1929, where the main focus of the research was the theory of business cycles.

Kuznets's initial academic research addressed "long waves" of economic development, prompted at the time by the Russian economist Nikolai Kondratieff. Kuznets conducted several analyses of America's historical business cycles and came to the unexpected conclusion that the long cycles Kondratieff had described did not actually exist.[5] With this analysis, Kuznets made a name for himself not only as an empiricist but also as a researcher who knew how to handle data that could be used to analyze the national income and national product. Thus, it was not surprising that the NBER approached Kuznets when, in the early 1930s, it was look-ing for an expert in national income accounting. Kuznets remained associated with the NBER until the 1950s. In 1930, Kuznets was appointed to the University of Pennsylvania, where he stayed until 1954. After a stint at Johns Hopkins University, he spent the years 1960 to 1971 at Harvard. His pupils included not only Milton Gilbert (of whom we will learn more) but also Milton Friedman, whose own empirical studies later played a pivotal role in replacing Keynesianism as the dominant form of economics.

Kuznets put forth his views on national income in the publications *National Income, 1929–1932* (1934), *National Income and Capital Formation, 1919–1935* (1937), *National Income and Its Composition, 1919–38* (1941), *National Product, War and Prewar* (1944), and *National Product in Wartime* (1945). However, it was the article "National Income," which Kuznets published in 1933 in the *Encyclopaedia of the Social Sciences*, that was decisive. Together with the study *National Income, 1929–1932*, conducted for Congress, it dominated the discussion about the method of national income accounting in America for years. Both texts were regarded as standard reference works. However, government recording of national income was later transferred to the Department of Commerce, which gradually distanced itself from Kuznets's approaches and moved more toward the Brit-ish system and methodology, as I will discuss further below.

In 1942, Kuznets joined the planning committee at the War Production Board, a unit President Roosevelt had set up to centralize the planning of armaments production and the associated supply of resources. The War Production Board analyzed the various areas of the economy in detail and, first and foremost, this included the recording of national income data.

Shortly after World War II, Kuznets attempted to develop a national accounts system for the Chinese government under Chiang Kai-shek in Nanking. He later abandoned the topic of national income entirely and placed greater focus on the determinants of growth. Like Colin Clark, Kuznets combined his investigations into growth with thoughts about trends in population growth, arguing in various essays that an increase in population could play an important role in generating greater output, as it facilitated technological change. And, like Clark, Kuznets assumed that it generally would be possible to feed an increasing global population without a reduction in the standard of living.

Kuznets was one of the generation of researchers who came to the United States from Europe—where they had experienced extreme political turmoil and had often been persecuted on account of their religious beliefs—and went on to dominate American economic science in the first half of the twentieth century. Many of them had received a sound middle-class education; moved at an early age in different cultural, linguistic, and political spheres; and, on account of their experience of totalitarian ideologies, had become skeptical of simplistic attempts to explain the world. They refused to be shackled to an ideological bandwagon, keeping their sights fixed on complexity and the respective historical context.[6]

Kuznets's work is characterized by extreme sensitivity to the quality of the data and a cautious approach to deducing laws from statistical observations.[7] In his 1955 essay on the link between growth and inequality, he impressively described the necessity of investigating general political conditions alongside economic and empirical evidence when analyzing socioeconomic circumstances. "It is inevitable that we venture into fields beyond those recognized in recent decades as economics proper," he wrote.[8] Economics should no longer be a science that just investigated market processes, in Kuznets's view; his was a political and social economics.

The disadvantage of such an approach was that it didn't lend itself well to simple and abstract models or to clear technocratic concepts and key terms—all necessary for swift and short-term political action. The same was true of Kuznets's ideas on national income. With his stance on empirical research and economics, he could not present a usable political arithmetic of national income accounting. That would not have fitted in with his approach to the field. As opposed to Clark, he did not want to produce a system that gave the state clear instructions on how to act and increase its power. National income and gross national product only became politically powerful figures once Kuznets's students discovered the possibility of influencing politicians; they threw their teacher's skepticism overboard and disregarded the complexity of his deliberations.

Despite his high academic standing, Kuznets had difficulty asserting himself in the field. In their 1995 biographical article, Vibha Kapuria-Foreman and Mark Perlman stated that, among economists, there was "profound ignorance" about Kuznets and his work. That was partially the case even during Kuznets's lifetime. Shortly before he was awarded an honorary doctorate by Princeton University, he met the prominent economist Jacob Viner on Nassau Street. When Viner heard of the forthcoming award, he asked Kuznets, surprised, "Whatever for?"[9]

NATIONAL INCOME AND
THE GREAT DEPRESSION

Staff at the NBER had first calculated the national income of the United States, on its own account, in the early 1920s, for the years 1909 to 1919. In 1926, the Federal Trade Commission produced its own estimate of national income. But the means for further statistical work by federal authorities were cut, and no further estimates were produced for the time being. As was the case elsewhere in the world, the concept of national income was not part of the public's perception or of political debates.

In 1931, the United States was in the midst of the Great Depression, and economic conditions were dire. Almost one in four American workers was unemployed, with part- and short-time work the rule. The banking system was in ruins, deflation was hampering economic expansion, and the fall in private consumption was threatening the very existence of many companies. In the agriculture sector, which provided a living for a quarter of all Americans, incomes had plummeted by half. No one, though, knew what exactly had happened in and to the country's economy since 1929.[10] Furthermore, the United States lacked reliable data to describe the overall economic situation.[11] For the most part, the existing data was years old and obsolete, unhelpful for conclusions about the current economic situation. Some politicians saw an urgent need for action.

At the instigation of Senator Robert M. La Follette Jr. from Wisconsin, the Senate set up a commission of inquiry to get an idea of the situation. High-ranking representatives from the railroads, the automotive and steel industries, banking, and universities, as well as other experts (among them, the head of the research department in the Department of Commerce, Frederic Dewhurst), were invited to join. Dewhurst clearly described the desolate state of economic and social statistics.[12] Although the Department of Commerce published thousands of tables and indexes for a number of goods, industrial sectors, production, and commerce, there was no information about trends in income and consumer spending by private households, and just as little about saving, investment, or the rise in living costs and prices. Dewhurst, however, was certain that it was possible to obtain the missing data and evaluate them using a coherent system. This aroused the interest of the committee.

SENATOR SHEPPARD: I ask whether it would be advisable to secure a complete picture of the economic situation which would be of benefit to the Government and to the people of the country?

MR. DEWHURST: In my opinion, it would be most desirable. May I add that a statistician is prejudiced in that he always wants more statistics. Statisticians are never satisfied. But I am impressed constantly with the requests for information that we get in the Department of Commerce, so many of which have to be answered to the effect that we do not know. So often we have to say we do not know, and nobody else knows, so far as we can tell.[13]

As a result, in June 1932, Resolution 220 (Estimates of National Income and Its Distribution), which declared the estimate of national income to be the task of government, was introduced to Congress. It tasked the Department of Commerce with presenting national income statistics, initially for the years 1929 to 1931. This involved calculating the contribution of different sectors to national income, and identifying the parts (wages, salaries, profits, pension payments, and so forth) that made up the income generated.[14]

In her history of the American national accounts, Carol Carson argues that although such a resolution may seem revolutionary, given how little attention had previously been paid to these measures, it wasn't really, as there had been growing political interest in national income statistics. That said, Carson fails to appreciate that the approach was unprecedented in the history of GDP. For the first time, it was the government that requested such statistical information, and from the outset, it not only recognized the political benefit of compiling these figures but also was aware of the need to check which figures were gathered, in what form.

Shortly after his statement to the commission, Dewhurst left the Department of Commerce. Since no one else was in a position to make the calculations, the department approached the NBER. Willford King had been responsible for national income accounting there. However, the institute's management had begun to have doubts about the methodical quality of his estimates, which, for example, included housework. Kuznets was asked to critically examine the methodology behind King's approach and to provide more credible calculations.[15] In "National Income," Kuznets presented his own definition and methodology of calculation. Robert La Follette's staff brought La Follette's attention to a preliminary draft version of Kuznets's article, which was making the rounds in Washington.

Kuznets was tasked with national income accounting for the years 1929 to 1931. He was assisted by two department staffers, both graduates of the University of Pennsylvania. One of these was Milton Gilbert, who from 1941 would head the national income recording program and would emerge as one of Kuznets's sharpest critics.

"NATIONAL INCOME" IN THE *ENCYCLOPAEDIA OF THE SOCIAL SCIENCES* (1933)

It was thanks to his brother that Kuznets—not well known among researchers for his work on national income—was entrusted with the entry for the *Encyclopaedia of the Social Sciences*. Salomon Kuznets was one of the editor's closest members of staff, and awarded the contract to Simon, who seized the opportunity to present his view of the topic.[16] His entry presented what was, until then, the most comprehensive methodological and theoretical statement on national income. As opposed to most of the other publications on national income, his was not aimed at an expert audience. It was written in a generally comprehensible way, and made do with few technical details. With this, Kuznets was able to get his views across to a wide audience.

For Kuznets, it was not only income (which could be calculated as consumption, its distribution, and the value of production) that made up the figure national income. He added a fourth category, "income enjoyed," or the sum total of all subjective feelings, which each individual has in his dual function as producer and consumer.[17] In so doing, Kuznets extended the range of interpretation of national income with a subjective component: the satisfaction resulting from one's own economic activity.[18] Such feelings, however, were not measurable, so in order to quantify national income, one had to concentrate on the cruder benchmarks of income received and consumed.

At first sight, Kuznets maintained, national income seemed to provide an objective survey of economic strength. It could be read as an index of production capacity and would enable a comparison of the productivity of different countries. The per capita income could be an indicator of a country's economic welfare, and if sufficient data was available, it would be possible to describe the trend over a longer period of time, to make statements about how much richer or poorer a country had become, and to show how income was distributed across certain groups in society. But Kuznets deliberately wrote in the conditional. He warned about overestimating the potential of this type of calculation: "However used, figures like those . . . appear to be quite serviceable; they seem to measure in comparable units something quite definite and significant. Further investigation reveals, however, that the clear and unequivocal character of such estimates is deceptive."[19]

Demonstrating the difficulties inherent in the method of calculation was important to him. In order to avoid misinterpretations or wishful thinking, one had to be familiar with the "gap" between what *can* be measured and what *should* be measured.[20] Kuznets saw national income as a sum that presented a snapshot of a particular moment in time, one that could in no way replace deeper analysis or render it superfluous.[21]

According to Kuznets, the purpose of the economic system was to provide the citizens of a country with goods and services. What was decisive in the recording of national income was the moment at which individuals in the economic cycle achieved their income. Kuznets had a clear and realistic concept: national income had to be thought of in terms of the incomes individuals get, and not as the total value of production. However, Kuznets realized that this definition didn't solve all problems with the measure. It was difficult to evaluate incomes for which no specific amount of money had been paid, and the concept of "income" was ambiguous, inasmuch as there were different motivations for achieving income. Individuals, for example, need an income in order to support themselves and maintain their standard of living. Companies, though, want to generate profits.

From these thoughts, Kuznets deduced what should be calculated as income and what should not: national income comprised the sum total of wages and salaries, pensions, interest, dividends, and so forth—any item, that is, with a measurable market price. The value of goods manufactured for one's own final consumption, without money being paid, or of services such as unpaid housework were not taken into consideration, although they directly benefited individuals. This was done for pragmatic reasons and resulted from the necessity to differentiate between economic activities and individuals' private lifestyles.[22] Such a dividing line could only be determined from country to country, and could shift over the course of time.[23] Comparing calculations of a country's national income made at different times, or comparisons between different countries, could be misleading. The national income of countries with a very disparate distribution of income also could hardly be compared. Furthermore, there was no objective criterion for how public authority services not traded on the free market should be valued, or whether the value of the goods produced should be calculated on a net or a gross basis. For observations conducted over a short period, the gross value was more accurate, because in this case the depreciation of capital was difficult to estimate.

Just how important it was for Kuznets to see national income as the entirety of concrete individual incomes and not simply as an abstract sum is also revealed by the fact that he did not stop at the aggregated recording of incomes. For him, the *distribution* of income also was an integral part of national income recording. He spent almost half of his *Encyclopaedia* entry on this. Because individual welfare was dependent on the level of income an individual had at her disposal, recording of national income had to be linked to a recording of income distribution. Only both, together, enabled statements about a country's welfare.

The recording of national income was therefore dependent on a social consensus as to what was meant by economic activity. Consequently, certain social and institutional structures influenced the way national income could and should be calculated. In different contexts, the term "national income" meant different things.

This applied to families as an economic unit as well.[24] Whereas in modern Western countries families no longer played any significant role in economic production (even if only for their own needs), in most parts of the world, families were still a constitutive element in the economic structure. The economic standing of families and household production not only changed over the course of time, as had been demonstrated in Europe, but also was different from region to region within a country. As such, the method of recording had to be adapted to the local circumstances in each case. Kuznets categorically ruled out a universal method for recording national income, possibly even worldwide, as an option.

THE OFFICIAL ESTIMATE OF 1934

The results of Kuznets's calculations were presented in 1934 as a Senate publication entitled *National Income, 1929–1932*.[25] It was an attempt to describe the entire activity of the economy from the income side, and the data painted a dramatic picture. National income had fallen by half, income from production had fallen by 70 percent, and income from construction had dropped by 80 percent. Only the public sector had grown. Wage earners had had to accept bigger cuts than salaried employees.[26]

As clear as the figures themselves were, Kuznets warned of the danger of overestimating their informative value. The report repeatedly stressed that different definitions inevitably lead to different results. This was particularly so in the case of the approach taken, which saw the market reflected in national income and thus accorded market prices a key role. However, Kuznets emphasized, no meaningful information about economic welfare could be gleaned without an accurate analysis of the distribution situation. Kuznets's overall assessment was that no conclusion about economic welfare could be drawn using the figures provided.

Kuznets was well aware of the dangers and political risk the compilation of his data involved. He warned:

The valuable capacity of the human mind to simplify a complex situation in a compact characterization becomes dangerous when not controlled in terms of definitely stated criteria. With quantitative measurements especially, the definiteness of the result suggests, often misleadingly, a precision and simplicity in the outlines of the object measured. Measurements of national income are subject to this type of illusion and resulting abuse, especially since they deal with matters that are the center of conflict of opposing social groups where the effectiveness of an argument is often contingent upon oversimplification.[27]

Kuznets used two definitions of national income. On the one hand, there was the "national income produced," and on the other, the "national income paid out." The difference was that national income produced included the amount companies saved—the difference between profits and payments in the form of wages and salaries, dividends, and interest rate payments. National income paid out referred solely to income channeled into production factors. The first measurement was therefore more comprehensive, as it took into account the part of the profits that was not paid out.

National income produced represented the value of the current production of goods and services after deducting depreciation, and was identical to the net national product at market prices. That, in turn, was defined as the income available for consumption and investment. In the course of the 1930s, this definition was gradually established in publications and, for reasons of simplicity, was subsequently referred to only as national product.

The report showed that, starting in 1930, companies had started dipping into savings. They either tapped their financial reserves and provisions or went into debt to carry on production, because costs were greater than their income. This meant that national income paid out was greater than national income produced—a clear, and numerically proven, sign of economic crisis.[28]

Following the publication for the Senate, Kuznets and his colleagues set about extending their calculations of national income further into the past, to gain a better understanding of the American economy's historical development processes. In 1937, Kuznets's book *National Income and Capital Formation, 1919–1935* appeared. Like the report, it addressed in detail questions of definition, with Kuznets comparing the concepts he used with other calculation models.

For Kuznets, national income was closely linked to the market economy—or at least to that economic system that in "economically advanced nations of recent times" was referred to as the market economy. Inasmuch as a market was the place where potential buyers and sellers meet, national income measured the net product of the activities realized on the market and excluded those activities conducted outside the market.[29]

INITIAL POLITICAL SUCCESS

The Department of Commerce made efforts to ensure that estimates were regularly made on behalf of the government, even after Kuznets stopped working for the department, in 1934. By that point, government agencies were more able to receive and collect data, and from then on the Department of Commerce calculated national income figures annually—although, for the first few years, due to an initial lack of employees, the results were available neither immediately nor on the desired scale. Because the income statistics included the transfers the state welfare system had been paying to the needy since the Great Depression, the data was of interest from both an economic and a sociopolitical point of view. Government facilities entrusted with social transfers, for example, resorted to them.

Politicians and the general public made more and more use of the official national income figures. In particular, the 50 percent drop in national income, expressed in figures in Kuznets's first report, was used as justification, from 1933 on, for the highly controversial public investment measures implemented as part of the New Deal. Because national income was a category that the government had recognized from the outset as being meaningful statistical information, it also quickly acquired a prominent place in political debates. The view that progress could be measured using national income soon became commonplace.

In the 1936 presidential election campaign, public use of the data was already so widespread that the incumbent, President Franklin D. Roosevelt, was able to refer in his speeches to the rise in national income in the previous four years in order to highlight the success of his economic policy.[30] In his annual budget message of 1938, Roosevelt then demanded: "We must start again on a long, steady, upward incline in national income."[31] As of that year, national income estimates were made monthly and thus were seen as statements about the current condition of the economy. Using the key figure of national income, it was also possible to illustrate macroeconomic phenomena at short notice.

KEYNES AND THE TRIUMPHAL FORWARD MARCH OF GROSS NATIONAL PRODUCT

The national income, which the Department of Commerce used to produce official government figures, was calculated using the Kuznets method and was independent of Keynesian theory. Nor was there any system of accounts, as was the case with Meade and Stone. Gradually, however, criticism of Kuznets's method of calculation began to emerge—not least among those associated with the government. An appreciable number of politicians and academics subscribed to Keynesianism and wanted information about relevant economic aggregates, which the Department of Commerce could not provide with its method of calculation. Hand in hand with this was the establishment of the concept of gross national product, precisely among the Keynesians in the government.

As early as 1934, in a project entitled "Distribution of Wealth and Income in Relation to Economic Progress," Clark Warburton from the Brookings Institution had attempted to calculate the value of all end products and services. He also was the first to call this gross national product.[32] Warburton's estimates included far more factors than the national income calculation used by Kuznets and others. Among other things, Warburton included government spending.

At the same time, the ideas of Keynesianism were becoming established in the United States. A group of economists from Harvard succeeded in convincing the government of the necessity for an active economic policy, and national income statistics had to enable the scope of the requisite public infrastructure measures to be determined.[33] Gross national product was first estimated for the National Defense Advisory Commission in 1940, though only from the production side; part of the process was an investigation of the extent to which increased defense spending would influence the economy.

For Kuznets, in the calculation of income, the focus was on the individual. The state featured only inasmuch as it made transfer payments. In the entry in the *Encyclopaedia of the Social Sciences,* the state received practically no mention. In his own works, Kuznets placed the focus on national income paid out—that is, private households' disposable income. Theoretically, in the calculation of national income, spending that reflected "economic civilization"—spending for armaments, infrastructure, and transport—had to be deducted. This spending was a necessary evil, which should be recorded as an interim product (i.e., intermediate consumption), but which was not available to end consumers for consumption. Colin Clark and Simon Kuznets rated state activity very similarly.

Viewed from this perspective, an increase in armaments production registered as a decline in national income. Before the United States entered World War II, the Office of Price Administration and Civilian Supply (OPACS)—entrusted with mobilizing resources for the war—strongly advocated such an increase, but it initially failed to push through its demands because increased state spending was expected to have such negative effects on national income.

OPACS thus had a vested interest in implementing Keynesianism. The authority relied on estimates of private consumption, private and public investment, and government spending—all aggregates, which played in outstanding role in Keynesian theory. The director of the Defense Economic Section of OPACS, Richard Gilbert, was the elder cousin of Milton Gilbert, Kuznets's student. Milton Gilbert was responsible for national income estimates in the Department of Commerce. Before the war, the two had been speechwriters for President Roosevelt, as had the Harvard economist John Kenneth Galbraith.

Richard Gilbert, who taught at Harvard, was one of the first American Keynesians. Roosevelt had initially thought little of Keynes's doctrines, but Gilbert was able to win him over to Keynesian theory. Gilbert had closely studied the British publications on national income accounting, particularly those by Meade and Stone, and immediately recognized that he could use this calculation logic to demonstrate that an increase in armaments production did not necessarily entail a prohibitive fall in national income.

When Keynes visited the United States in 1941, he exchanged opinions and ideas with OPACS staffers (including some of his former students) and their director, Richard Gilbert. At the time, OPACS was working on its own estimate of gross national product. Keynes and Gilbert discussed the structure of national income and the method used for its calculation.[34] The result was an estimate of gross national product, presented by OPACS in 1941, which calculated the effects of higher spending on armaments and included public expenditure spending. It was an explicit attempt to establish a different method of calculation from that of Kuznets. Keynes was very positive about the study and said it was the work of young economists, who no longer subscribed to old frames of mind.

Milton and Richard Gilbert were close friends and shared an apartment in Washington. Richard convinced his younger cousin of the idea of a gross national product, such that the latter, upon his appointment as head of the research department in the Department of Commerce, converted national income accounting to gross national product accounting supported by Keynesian theory.[35] With this, in 1942 Kuznets and the Department of Commerce went their separate ways.

The main distinguishing feature between the two accounting approaches was the role accorded to the state. This wasn't a gradual change; it was a totally new way of interpreting economic procedures. Unlike the British system, in the United States, production and not taxable income was the deciding parameter. When the economy switched from being war- to peacetime-based, an accurate estimate of the strength of American production was politically more relevant than the question of how much disposable income households possessed.

GROSS NATIONAL PRODUCT
PROVES ITS WORTH

The U.S. entry into World War II accelerated the concentration on production. The attack on Pearl Harbor in late 1941 led to a drastic increase in the defense budget: President Roosevelt envisaged spending $56 billion on armaments in 1942; one year earlier the figure had stood at $13 billion. Such an extreme increase would fundamentally change the economic structure of the United States.

It was unclear what concrete effects such an increase would have. National income had grown along with the rise in armaments spending, and now stood above the 1929 level, but many economists suspected that such a dramatic increase would cause private consumption to fall, given the need for resources and other goods. However, there were no statistics that accurately itemized the products and services that made up the national product, so it was difficult to tell which areas would be affected by a material shortage. Though national income provided a picture of the general condition of the economy, it could not show where production bottlenecks might occur and so could not point to possibilities for subsidies.

There was, however, enormous political interest in invalidating the still prevalent opinion that increasing spending on and production of armaments inevitably led to a decrease in national income. In 1942, Milton Gilbert published an extensive study on the topic, which played a pivotal role in replacing national income with gross national product as the established parameter in American politics. Gilbert's view was that basic statements could be made about the structural transformation an increase in defense spending would cause, and from this, recommendations for action could be deduced. However, he considered the existing statistics to provide little in the way of information. The initial stage of the war mobilization, he wrote, was akin to a situation in which one tenders for something without knowing the capacity of one's own plant or the financial means available.[36]

Gilbert first ascertained that the rise in annual defense spending that had already taken place—from less than $3 billion in 1940 to more than $13 billion in 1941—had not led to a reduction in private consumption. On the contrary, private consumption had reached record levels, as had national income, which during the same period had increased from $75 billion to $104 billion.

The deciding question was how much of the total product would be left over for private, civilian consumption if the state's planned defense spending were executed.[37] To answer this question, the general opinion among those calculating national income was that state spending on armaments and defense had to be deducted from the estimated national income; the amount remaining was all that was available for private consumption. From the figures available, the conclusion was that the private sector would have to forgo a third of its current consumption for the president's armament plans to be realized. However, Gilbert found calculations of this nature misleading. They led, he said, to totally distorted picture that did not do justice to the American economy's production capacity.[38]

The simple distinction between planned war-related and peace-related spending formed the basis of Gilbert's recalculation. He argued that, as an aggregate of income, national income could not be linked to spending on armaments. After all, he opined, the armaments budget was used for purchasing goods and services at market prices. As such, the statistical factor to which spending on armaments should be compared was the value of all goods and services produced in a specific period, valued at market prices. National income, on the other hand, merely indicated the net value of production, expressed as the sum total of the incomes of the various production factors.

According to Gilbert, in order for national income to become a measure of production at market prices, one first had to clarify how the taxes that companies paid on their profits, before paying wages, salaries, interest, and so on, were to be included in the calculation. Because of these taxes, the selling price of goods and services could not be identical to the factor costs incurred during their production (such as, for example, the income that is paid to the production factors in the form of wages and salaries). And because part of the income went to the state through taxation, the state had to be regarded as an income recipient and the relevant contribution of taxes to national income should be added to the overall measure of national income, to equal the value of the market prices for goods and services. This was, then, still a net value.

For a comparison with armaments spending, however, Gilbert proposed using the gross value—in other words, not deducting depreciation. The approaches used for calculating depreciation were methodically vague and flawed, said Gilbert, and in addition, the depreciation on a cutting-edge armaments industry that emerged through the transformation of the economy would carry scarcely any weight. Thus, the gross value would be more accurate than any measure that attempted to deduct the cost of depreciation, no matter how this was done.[39] The simplest reason, however, was that if one looked at market prices, the cost of depreciation was accounted for (in the case of armaments as well).

Gilbert called the resulting figure gross national product or gross national expenditure. In addition to the value of the goods and services produced by the private sector at market prices, it also included the value of the goods and services produced by the state.[40] Gross national product, estimated this way, was 25 percent higher than estimates of the national income.[41]

These calculations allowed Gilbert to reveal the composition of spending for the years 1939 to 1941, and to estimate it for 1942. Gradually increasing spending on armaments, he showed, had not led to a crowding out in the economy but to a significant increase in overall production—not just on account of increased state spending but also because employment, the average working week, and productivity had risen. The beginning of the transformation of the economy from peacetime to war requirements had increased the proportion of industries producing extremely high-quality goods.

Given this situation, Gilbert painted a different picture of the increased defense spending scenario. From the planned $56 billion of spending on armaments, he deducted the previous year's spending, leaving him with a figure of around $42 billion. How could the country afford such an increase in spending? According to Gilbert, the answer was that the U.S. economy had by no means reached its production limit. There were still many people out of work, who could be integrated in the production process. The number of weekly working hours also could still be increased, and unutilized industrial capacity was also available.[42] According to Gilbert's estimates, reaching the government's production targets would push gross national product from $115 billion in 1941 to $132 billion in 1942.

An underlying assumption was that that the armament plans could only be put into practice if civil goods were converted into war supplies. But this conversion alone, Gilbert maintained, would not suffice to produce the target number of tanks, airplanes, and ships. The possibilities for conversion in the consumer goods industry (such as cars, electrical goods, or clothing) were extremely limited, although there was greater possibility in the case of capital goods (such as factories, machines, trucks, and agricultural equipment). Thus, the production of certain goods would have to be halted or reduced, though the possible expansion of production was decisive.

After deducting state spending on armaments (which, according to Gilbert, would be only $53 billion, due to individual adjustments), only around $79 billion of the projected $132 billion in gross national product would be available for other spending, including government spending not related to armaments—far less than the $102 billion still available for that purpose in 1941, but far more than supporters of national income accounting were predicting. The private sector would therefore have to restrict its consumption habits, because the production of goods that were not essential for the war would decline—although not by a third, as previously assumed, but by a fifth, at most.

Calculation of gross national product not only demonstrated that implementing the armaments plans would have less dramatic consequences than was feared but also made it clear that this spending could be increased. For Gilbert, expansion and conversion were the most important political concepts for satisfying the demands of the armaments industry. A large proportion of planned spending on armaments could be offset by increased production and by private individuals' renunciation of investments and durable consumer goods. This information was of enormous importance for politicians; it meant people hardly had to do without the goods and services that covered their basic needs, such as clothing, housing, and food.

Furthermore, calculation of gross national product helped to identify important key indicators in the fight against inflation. According to the Keynesian theory of inflation prevalent at the time, the inflation gap was an important tool for calculating the risk of inflation. The concept of the inflation gap was based on the idea that inflation occurs when the demand for goods and services exceeds the supply—when there is a gap between supply and demand. The information about taxes, consumption, and savings in gross national product calculations was a decisive help in calculating the danger of inflation and revealed how taxation measures could lower income and reduce demand.[43]

Beginning in May 1942, the Department of Commerce published estimates of gross national product in its *Survey of Current Business*, along with in-depth tables covering the ratio of gross national product to national income, the distribution of gross national product by expenditure and income, and how income was spent. Soon after, gross national product using constant prices was calculated and published quarterly.[44]

However, the new concept of gross national product did not establish itself automatically and on its own. Privately owned companies, in particular, didn't know what they were meant to do with such figures. So, in 1944, in the business journal *Dun's Review*, Milton Gilbert aimed to convey to a wider audience the advantages of calculating gross national product and to demonstrate that it was a source of important information not only for the state but also for companies.[45]

War requirements were the reason for this focus on gross national product. The key questions were about the American economy's war potential and about how expanding armaments production might affect inflation. Answering these questions required not only information about the goods produced but also figures about income and how it was being spent. That, Gilbert said, was exactly the need that calculating gross national product fulfilled. Though national income enabled an estimate of purchasing power, it did not provide an answer to the questions that arose during the war. For this, production data was needed, for both the private and the state sector. Gross national product was nothing other than the measure of this production. By combining it with a calculation of the way income was spent, a bird's-eye view of the workings of the economy emerged.

Gilbert declared the switch to gross national product a success, because the government was now using statistics as the basis of its planning and was able to identify the available potential for increased armaments production.[46] However, he noted, gross national product statistics were also meaningful in times of peace—for the state as much as for the private economy. The statistics contained important economic data and provided companies with essential information about the state of the economy as a whole and the way it was developing. According to Gilbert, more and more companies were using gross national product statistics for their own market and economic analyses.

Toward the end of the war, gross national product surveys finally replaced national income accounting as the main statistics for analyzing the economic situation. In his budget speech to Congress, in January 1945, President Roosevelt spoke of gross national product for the first time. It was already apparent that, when the war was over, the American economy would face another major challenge: the retransformation of the economy from wartime to peacetime.

During the war, government spending was responsible for almost half of the gross national product—almost one in five Americans was in the military, and most of the workforce was employed either directly or indirectly in the armaments industry or in the production of civil consumer goods that were important for the war. In the postwar era, the goal was to create enough jobs and, after years of low consumer and investment spending, stimulate domestic demand and private investment to make full employment possible. In his budget speech, Roosevelt made it clear that the renewed restructuring of the economy could not be achieved without a suitable statistical basis: "Statistical information concerning business activities and markets, employment and unemployment, incomes, expenditures, and savings is urgently needed as a guide for economic policies during the remainder of the war and during the reconversion and postwar period."[47]

CALCULATIONS IN WAR AND PEACE

Milton Gilbert had made it clear that, from his point of view, calculating gross national product was by no means a tool that could be used only in wartime. It provided the state with an indispensable basis for decision making, and so should be conducted by government bodies on a permanent basis. Research institutes such as the National Bureau of Economic Research and independent economists like Simon Kuznets had no further role to play.

Kuznets, however, did not admit defeat without putting up something of a fight. Even when the war was still on, he attempted to promote his views on national income. In his book *National Product, War and Prewar* (1944) and in a remarkable piece of writing entitled *National Product in Wartime*, which appeared in spring 1945, Kuznets considered gross national product and how it is calculated during war and during peace. He defined national product as the total net contribution of economic activity of a nation. For Kuznets, the term "contribution" was decisive: *For what end was something made? What was the objective?* The other definitions, on the other hand, were relatively unproblematic: "economic activity" referred to purely economic procedures; "total" meant having to find a way by which qualitatively different final products were given comparable and additive weights. And the restriction to one nation showed that the ultimate purpose of the economic activity referred to one's own country and that, initially, there was no desire for international comparability.[48]

What purpose did war production serve? Did it play a role in satisfying end consumers' needs? Could it thus be recorded statistically, like all other consumer goods? Or, did the existing capital stock of the country increase through armaments production, such that the possibility of future goods production increased? Was the objective behind defense of the country the same as that behind the production of consumer goods, or was it something completely different?

As desirable as it was to find a single measure with which one could track the trends in an economy over the course of time and make comparisons with other countries, getting to a single measure could only be done at the cost of a reduction in complexity, which would make it impossible to gain a realistic picture of the economy. Every method had advantages and drawbacks. The national product, as Kuznets put it, was "a concept . . . that implies answers to problems over which social philosophers have wrangled from time immemorial."[49] The methodological challenges and inaccuracies in data rendered the measure far less valuable than it might appear.

In any case, the method used for calculation of national product had to be different during war than in peacetime. It was difficult enough to agree on the parameters for the measurement of the national product in peacetime; an extreme situation such as a war only served to make the problem worse, as it was then hardly possible to differentiate between intermediate and final products, or between gross and net. During wartime, not only the role of the state in the economic process changed; a war fundamentally changed the ultimate purpose of all economic policy. In peacetime, that is, the aim of all economic policy was to supply consumers with goods and services. As such, the ultimate purpose of all economic activity was satisfying human needs. In wartime, however, the goal was to make as many goods and services available as were needed to maintain what had already been achieved and to win the war as quickly as possible. In peacetime, the goal was to produce goods for the people; in wartime, the goal was for people to produce goods to win the war.

Recognizing this key difference, Kuznets proposed two different calculations. In the one, war production was seen as an increase in the existing capital stock. In the other, it was seen as another final product. The decision between the two depended on whether one took a short- or a long-term perspective.

In wartime, in the short term, all of a country's needs can be geared toward war production. The military conflict dominates all economic activity, so it is logical to count war material as a final product. The same applies to the differentiation between gross and net: in the short term, net amounts are irrelevant for politicians, who have to decide on plans for further war production. In the long term, on the other hand, one must allow for the depreciation of capital—wear and tear on capital goods and the aging of factories—to better illustrate the processes in the economy.[50] The gross value of all output is important for decision makers during a war but is inadequate for long-term comparative observations.

Over the long term and in peacetime, armaments and war materials cannot be seen as consumer goods. Rather, their production must be viewed as an increase in the existing capital. Different calculations of national income can thus be explained by the fact that, in war and in peacetime, the function of the state and the production of war material have to be evaluated differently.

However, Kuznets made it clear that the long-term, peacetime aim of all economic policy—the provision of consumers with goods and services—was not a generally valid specification that transcended time. Were a country, for example, to enter into a planned process of industrialization over three or four decades, to catch up with more developed countries, the aim of economic policy could be the accumulation of capital goods. Conversely, in a highly developed country, the maximization of existing goods might cease to be the ultimate objective of economic policy; leisure time and dabbling in the arts, for instance, might be more desirable, and economic activities could be subordinated to the goal of enjoying noneconomic activities.[51]

Ultimately, Kuznets addressed the elementary question of what national product can actually measure, and what it cannot:

> From many viewpoints, the provision of goods to consumers is a subsidiary rather than a primary aim of economic activity. If the functioning of the economic system is judged by its contribution to social welfare at large, if some idea of good life is the touchstone, then both provision of goods to consumers and any other immediate purpose of economic activity will be subordinate, and the entire calculation of national product, if calculation is still possible, will be different. No longer an economic concept, national product will become a concept with a broader frame of reference. If the social philosophy of recent years which . . . tends to subordinate it to some idea of a good life, of national glory, or of some other nebulous criterion deemed superior, is adopted, the net contribution of economic activity will have to be measured on the basis of the new and extra-economic goals.[52]

For Kuznets, the Department of Commerce's calculations of gross national product were unacceptable. Because they recorded all government spending as final products, they made government spending a variable, which could be changed by political decision making. Gross national product thus could not be seen as a specific, impartial methodology with which production could be calculated during wartime, because it accorded the state a major function in the economic system. An approach of this nature did not give an indication of the net contribution made by all economic policy because, by definition, there had to be cases of double counting. It was a method of calculation that gave particular weight to the government and to its influence on national product.[53]

In a review of Kuznets's *National Product, War and Prewar*, Milton Gilbert and others maintained that the proposals and calculations made by his former teacher were totally unsuitable for solving economic problems, whether in war or in peacetime. Pushing the view of the Department of Commerce, as a government authority, against Kuznets, a private researcher, was very important to Gilbert. The influence that the National Bureau of Economic Research still exerted on the method for calculating national income was a thorn in Gilbert's side. In his opinion, there were still too many who followed the NBER and who considered Kuznets's method plausible and practicable.[54]

Kuznets defended his point of view against Gilbert's criticism. As usual, he was particularly clear on the question of what statistical data could achieve and what it could not. The war was an extraordinary and extreme event, said Kuznets, which could not easily be addressed using peacetime concepts. National product accounting was needed in order to understand what was going on in the economy. However, according to Kuznets, one had to be aware that politicians could derive no recommended course of action from these calculations. All such calculations could do was tentatively define politicians' scope of action.[55] National product accounting could better identify a problem, but it could not provide a solution. Kuznets thought that this accounting should stimulate discussion of economic processes, such that the calculations themselves were repeatedly questioned. For this reason, he wanted his proposals to be seen not as a replacement for, but rather as an addition to the Department of Commerce's calculations.

THE CONFLICT OVER ACCOUNTS

In September 1944, representatives of the United States, Canada, and Great Britain met to harmonize the method of calculating national income. Simon Kuznets was not even invited to attend.

The discussion was dominated by Richard Stone, who was able to demonstrate to the Americans the logic behind his accounts system. Even at this first meeting, it became evident that the United States would gravitate toward the British method of calculation and thus effectuate a basic international consensus with regard to the accounts system.[56] Those attending the meeting emphasized that the objective was to bring transparency to economic transactions conducted by three groups: individuals, the state, and companies. It was, therefore, less to do with disclosing a specific figure and more with a *system* that revealed the connection between the individual aggregated figures. In particular, they dissociated themselves from attempts to use national income as a basis for calculating economic welfare.[57] In 1947, the Department of Commerce then presented its own accounts system, the national income and product accounts, based on Meade's and Stone's Keynesian system.[58]

It was clear to Kuznets as well that, in principle, a system of accounts was suitable for documenting transactions among economic entities, thereby providing an overview of economic activities.[59] It was thus possible to outline the function and importance of specific areas of the economy, investigate how they behaved with regard to trends in the overall aggregate, and identify growth patterns over the course of time. Kuznets, however, was in complete disagreement with the Department of Commerce's accounts system. In March 1948, he made his displeasure clear in an article in the *Review of Economics and Statistics*.[60] In the same issue, Gilbert and others responded to Kuznets's accusations and politely but forcefully contradicted him.

Kuznets maintained that the department's accounts system lacked any clear statement about the basis on which the method of calculation was determined. The unstated basis, as Kuznets saw it, was production, instead of the ultimate purpose of economic policy: the provision of goods for consumers. The system prioritized the means rather than the end goal. This being the case, the new purpose of all economic policy was the production of goods; the department had moved the focus from the consumer side to the production side. In this, Kuznets saw the fundamental difference with his own approach, and this difference was more than an argument about terminology. It was a completely different methodological and philosophical approach. Only time, Kuznets said, would tell which approach was more appropriate or could be of greater help in understanding changes to economic and social structures. Furthermore, in the way the department's accounts were compiled, Kuznets saw a very real danger—a system that was highly prone to misunderstandings and misuse.[61]

For Kuznets, this system of accounts in no way determined the point in the economic cycle at which the calculation should begin. Instead, all he saw in the calculations was expediency motivated by suppositions. But a system of accounts of this nature was not helpful, he said. It was like a notebook with empty pages—anyone could decide what to write in it.[62]

From Kuznets's point of view, the position of public authorities was particularly problematic. The Department of Commerce equated the state with consumers. This undermined one of Kuznets's principles: national income was meant to record individual consumption, and the state had to be left out. The state and its needs could only be equated with the needs of individual citizens if all state spending and activities that affected the economy were available to final consumers in the form of goods and services. In reality, though, some state spending benefited companies, and some spending that served social cohesion (such as spending on health care or education) could not be recorded as a consumable final product. Indeed, even if one saw the state as a producer of goods, not all state spending could be counted as a final product; a lot of what the state commissioned had to be booked as intermediate consumption in the production process. According to Kuznets, the department's approach inevitably led to double counts and prevented the comparison of measured data over time.

Furthermore, he said, it was incomprehensible why certain elements had been included in the Department of Commerce's accounts system but others had not. Instead of using theoretical deliberations to determine what was meant by income streams and economic transactions, all one had to do was take a closer look at how final consumers defined such terms. In any case, the accounts system posed the risk of a one-sided concentration on monetary flows, from which conclusions were drawn about the circulation of goods, without more closely observing the flow of goods outside the monetary zone.

In their response to Kuznets's criticism, Gilbert and his peers declared that they had the greatest of admiration for Kuznets's pioneering work, but between the lines was the sense that they wanted to assign Kuznets a place in the national income accounting history books, rather than taking him seriously as an equal partner in the current discussion.[63] As the systems of accounts were harmonized internationally between Great Britain and the United States, Kuznets became isolated among national income statisticians. His critics singled out, in particular, his claim to have identified the ultimate purpose of all economic activity; this introduced a "moral dimension" into the method of calculating the national income that, they said, had no place there. Gilbert and his peers referred explicitly to William Petty. It was their aspiration to continue his legacy.[64]

Indeed, with the official recording of national income and gross national product by the Department of Commerce, political arithmetic as Petty had first imagined it was implemented in an almost ideal way. A data system had been established to give the government a picture of economic activity from which recommendations for action could be deduced. Kuznets's critical interjections went unheard because they opposed the creation of a political arithmetic system. Kuznets was replaced by the defenders of political arithmetic, for whom gross national product accounting was not a matter for researchers but for government.

5

WAR, KIDNAPPING, AND DATA THEFT

Germany

As far as surveying national income was concerned, Germany was a latecomer. This was, of course, partly because Germany was not politically unified into a single country until 1871. Before that, it was made up of dozens of sovereign territories, each with its own head of state, currency, tax laws, and statistical offices. Although numerous national income statistics had been compiled for the various small German states during the nineteenth century (on the basis of income data from tax statistics), the calculations were made only irregularly and mostly unofficially, and the available data was considered insufficient. Moreover, the German economists' guild doubted that the figures were of any use. British and French attempts to quantify national income were likewise deemed of little utility to them.

In fact, it seemed as though such calculations could be highly risky. In 1870, Prussia and a coalition of German states went to war with France. Otto von Bismarck, the Prussian chancellor, used the war as a pretext to forge a unified German state, the German Reich, under Prussian hegemony. In addition to defeating France militarily and taking the Emperor Napoleon III hostage, Bismarck seized every possible opportunity to humiliate France. He founded the new German Reich at Versailles, and he imposed exorbitant reparations payments on France. To determine the sum that would economically debilitate the country for years, Bismarck used French estimates of national income. International experts considered these estimates to be inflated. Yet, because they came from French statisticians, Bismarck was able to invoke them and, in so doing, deliberately dupe the French into the bargain.[1]

It was not until 1899 that an estimate of national income was computed for the entire German Reich. However, this was based solely on a rough extrapolation of a few regional income statistics. It had little significance.[2]

It was economist Karl Helfferich, who would later become secretary for the Treasury of the German Reich and member of the executive board of Deutsche Bank, who presented the first comprehensive national income estimate for the German Reich, in 1913. As had been the case in all other historical attempts to calculate national income, his endeavor was not commissioned by the government. Helfferich based his analyses on tax estimates. With his calculations, which covered the period 1896 to 1912, he sought to study economic development during the reign of Wilhelm II, and in the best tradition of Petty's political arithmetic, he compared his findings with figures from Britain and France. Considering average per capita income, Helfferich noticed that Germany had seemingly overtaken France, in economic terms, during the preceding decades but that it still lagged significantly behind Britain. Helfferich is praised as a pioneer in Paul Studenski's classic history of national income calculation, and he endeavored to present data evidencing the Reich's constant, stable economic progress.[3]

Helfferich died in 1942, but in the final years of his life as a conservative politician, he contributed considerably to the political destabilization of the young Weimar Republic. His paper *Fort mit Erzberger* (Do Away with Erzberger!) (1919) paved the way for a mind-set that condoned the murder of Finance Minister Matthias Erzberger, who, as an official envoy of the German government, was forced to sign the armistice with the Allies in Compiègne in 1918, which ended the fighting of World War I. In Germany, the signing of the armistice was viewed by conservatives as treason and among the voices calling for Erzberger's death, Helfferich's was one of the loudest.

The statistics of the German Reich were not as advanced as those in other European countries, with regard to many economically relevant data collections (such as unemployment statistics, information on prices and salaries, or details on household consumption), and until the beginning of the Weimar Republic, the government was unable to draw a clear picture of economic activities. This can be primarily attributed to private sector resistance to the necessary surveys, opposition that was especially pronounced from the nineteenth century onward. Businesses were not required to disclose the information required to compile economic statistics. Accordingly, the statistical material available was sparse. As Adam Tooze notes in his history of German economic statistics in the early twentieth century, Germany during the Reich was anything but a strong state with regard to statistics.[4] Where information was collected, it was considered secret and classified.

Moreover, the Imperial Statistical Office, which had been founded in 1872, had to contend not only with the resistance of industry but also with the problems presented by German federalism. Germany had been unified, but it remained a federation of semiautonomous regions that didn't take well to bullying from the central government in Berlin. Indeed, the former individual states (all with their own statistical offices) guarded the information concerning their regions as though it were secret, or tried to use it to their advantage in Berlin. In addition, prior to World War I, economic and social statistics were not treated as separate fields. Until that time, there was likewise no special department in the Statistical Office that was responsible for economic statistics. The economy as an independent unit of analysis was still without significance.[5] Little importance was attached to official statistics when planning political processes; they did not have priority, and for a long time statistical offices were underfunded.

Even the outbreak of World War I did not change this. On the contrary, because the conflict was initially expected to be a short one, long-term planning appeared unnecessary, and most statistical surveys were canceled. Nonetheless, the major industrial corporations were aware of the greater need for planning. Walther Rathenau, director of the industrial company AEG in Berlin, established his own system of recording and controlling industrial raw materials requirements. Because Rathenau considered the official data worthless, the wartime Raw Materials Department, founded on his initiative, operated completely independently of the Imperial Statistical Office.[6]

German industry, however, continued to be uneasy about granting state agencies access to their processes and books. In order to make war planning more efficient, a duty of disclosure was introduced in 1917. Henceforth, firms were obliged to provide data, on pain of penalties. That, too, was met with resistance and, at least for the postwar period, businesses hoped to see a return to the days when they could retain their information for themselves.[7]

Compared to the German Reich, the Weimar Republic, created after Germany had lost the war, placed more emphasis on economic policy—and even created an economic ministry, for the first time in German history. The new significance of economic policy is evident in the fact that, from the very beginning, the president of the Weimar Republic, Friedrich Ebert, demanded monthly reports on the status of the economy.[8]

The sudden, strong political demand for statistical data can be explained by the simple fact that such information was urgently needed. It was imperative to know exact figures if the country was to address the problems of demobilization; stimulate economic activity, which was so necessary; reintegrate the German economy into global trade flows; combat hunger; and service the emerging, unprecedented reparations demanded by the Allies in the 1919 Treaty of Versailles, which named Germany as the country mainly responsible for the war. The principal problem, however, was that these figures had never been ascertained.

The state of the economy was a great unknown; the "vacuum of knowledge was almost complete."[9] There was no usable indicator for inflation; trade data was incomplete; unemployment figures were considered unreliable; and information on the employment rate, production, and income was missing. Yet, statistics on prices and income were particularly important. Prices furnished information about the cost of living, and income data provided information about how many people were living below the poverty line. Both sets of data had been given somewhat second-rate treatment under the Wilhelmine administration. The precise level of industrial revenue was unknown. Previous attempts to determine wage and salary levels had failed in the face of fierce opposition from industry and businesspeople, who feared that the results could furnish the Social Democrats with arguments.[10]

Now this data was to be gathered at the government's request, using sophisticated new social science methods. Shortly after the war, many municipalities had compiled their own cost-of-living index, but there was no national index at this time. When it was finally calculated, in 1920, it emerged that the cost of living had risen thirteenfold compared to the prewar period. The so-called Reichsindex was compiled regularly from then on, but industrial associations again repeatedly sought to sabotage it. For example, representatives of the textile industry refused to provide information on the cost of clothing; conversely, the absence of this information was cited as proof of the lack of credibility of the index, which clearly underestimated the costs for the working population.[11] From the mid-1920s onward, however, the

Reichsindex became a set of statistical data that also made political waves, as the parties sought to use the data collected for their own purposes.

It proved even more difficult to collect data on wages and salaries. The corresponding surveys were enthusiastically supported by the trade unions but continued to meet with strong resistance from large-scale industry, which called for a boycott, and whose influence meant the political decision in the Reichstag was delayed. With the onset of inflation in 1922, the figures that had been collected became worthless. Only after the period of hyperinflation ended could officials begin to collect meaningful statistics once again. Gathering data on income remained politically sensitive, however. This was, not least, a result of the increasing concentration of the German economy into corporate groups; these groups not only created unclear ownership structures but also did all they could to conceal key earnings data. The few surveys that were nonetheless conducted for individual industrial sectors showed a large gap between the wages negotiated and those actually paid.

The foundation of the Institute for Business-Cycle Research (Institut für Konjunkturforschung, or IfK) in 1925 represents a decisive caesura in the development of statistics and, accordingly, of national income statistics of the Weimar Republic. It was initiated by the director of the Reich Statistical Office, Ernst Wagemann. The institute, as headed by Wagemann, was intended to bring studies on the theory of economic monitoring and business cycles together with empirical research; collect, evaluate, and analyze data; and publish the findings and statistics in order to enable conclusions to be drawn about the state of the economy. Moreover, it later identified trends and forecast developments, things the Reich Statistical Office was not allowed to do by law—its role was to gather raw data, not play with it. Wagemann, instead, wished to combine expertise in economic statistics with a stronger influence on politics. The National Bureau of Economic Research in New York was one of the institute's role models.[12] What was characteristic of the IfK, however, was that it was attached to the Reich Statistical Office and thus was still part of official statistics, even if it acted like an independent research institute.

The IfK published its business-cycle, market, country, and sector analyses in various forms, first quarterly and then also weekly. The visual format of the data, with graphs and diagrams, was extremely progressive for the time and was adopted by the press.[13] Whereas economics had previously been an academic discipline, somewhat removed from politics, it was now being attributed a new practical relevance. Academics and government officials alike now thought that economic research should explicitly serve economic policy. People expected the institute to use data surveys and various indexes to describe the state of the economy and to predict its development, in the same way barometers were used to forecast the weather (this approach was known as the "Harvard barometer method" at the time)—a hope that could hardly become a reality, given the many different parameters. Wagemann was also, as Adam Tooze describes in detail, strongly influenced by Joseph Schumpeter's studies on business cycles and understood economic activities as a system of interlocking flows of goods and money. He conceived of a system of algebraic relations designed to enable these flows to be recorded statistically. In doing so, he came rather close to the Keynesian representation of national accounts that was later to prevail, without seeing a crucial variable in national income. Beginning in 1926, the institute reported its calculation of national income. This was a political issue. On the one hand, the funds available for reparations payments still needed to be gauged; on the other, representatives of employers and employees argued over how the overall income should be distributed more fairly. The IfK's calculation also was based on tax data, which was now more easily accessible, given that a universal income tax had been introduced in the Weimar Republic. The national income data was an important component of the institute's economic analysis, but because it was not a political control parameter, it was not published as official figures of the Reich Statistical Office.

National income was still a highly contentious concept among German economists at this time. At the annual conference of the economists' association Verein für Socialpolitik in Vienna, in 1926, heated debate broke out on the sense and nonsense of such surveys. Although several of the statisticians present cautiously pointed out that the national income calculation could improve knowledge, the critical voices prevailed. Not only did they dislike certain methodical definitions, such as that of income, but also the majority of professionals present vehemently rejected the fundamental idea that the complexity of economic relationships can be reduced to a single number. One of them summed up: "Following our criticism the last vestiges of respect towards attempts to state a simple sum for national income and national wealth must no doubt have evaporated. These attempts only have value for cheap political propaganda."[14]

This kind of critical stance did not disappear quickly. Even in the late 1930s, Schumpeter, who was teaching in the United States, reiterated the skepticism about national income that was widespread among economists: "The familiar difficulties which we all experience in defining National Income are of course due to the fact that it is not a technical term wedded to one definite use but a word of common parlance that is loosely used for a great many purposes which cannot be served equally well by a single definition."[15]

It wasn't until 1932 that the Reich Statistical Office compiled an official, comprehensive estimate of national income, which was primarily intended to describe the population's standard of living.[16] Income statistics referred to the years 1891 to 1913 and 1925 to 1931. The year 1913 was particularly interesting for statisticians, because it could serve as a basis both for estimating war damage and for comparison with even older data. The statistics were continued into 1938.

The resulting data on income distribution was among the most precise in the world. Yet it continued to be calculated only with the aid of the income method and was of only historical interest. National income figures were not seen by politicians as a suitable value for planning or forecasting, but simply showed how income had developed over the previous years.

What was missing for the complete statistical recording of economic activity was data on industrial output. Whereas regular comprehensive industrial surveys were conducted in Britain and the United States, this proved problematic in

Germany, for the aforementioned reasons. Wagemann began preparations for the first production census, which was to be conducted in the late 1920s, in order to enable the comparison of production data with national income data and the compilation of comprehensive national accounts. Although the planning took so long that the nascent global economic crisis made it impossible to continue with the industrial census, Wagemann, a gifted political networker, succeeded in allaying the historical doubts about statistics among entrepreneurs and industrialists. He positioned the institute, on whose board of trustees key industrial representatives sat, as an institution that was able to produce *credible* and *reliable* data and could therefore offer important *independent* and *scientific* bases for decision making, removed from the political conflicts of the day. In return, the industrial and entrepreneurial representatives provided the institute with their data, at least from time to time.

For a long time, Wagemann adhered to the business-cycle theory, stating that the economy was subject to a natural wave pattern. This is why, like many others, he did not believe the Great Depression entailed a structural crisis. Indeed, until 1932, the IfK expected the economy to soon recover of its own volition;[17] only then did the institute go on record saying that direct public invention in the economic cycle could be an option to smooth out economic imbalances.[18] National income was accorded a special role in the cycle analysis, but its increase was generally attributed to the fact that more jobs had been created and the economy was stabilizing.

The institute did not live up to the claim that it would be able to use economic data collection to precisely forecast future economic development, even if data analysis had advanced and led to new, empirically based findings. Although economic data received ever more public and political attention in the course of the crisis, the IfK itself became involved in an open dispute with Chancellor Brüning's government (from 1930 to 1932, during the height of the economic crisis) about whether the crisis was to be overcome through an expansive demand policy by the government (which the institute supported) or by deflation (as Brüning and his advisers intended). Moreover, the institute's position as the extended arm of the Reich Statistical Office, and thus as the virtually uncontested supplier of economic data, was politically controversial. The Nazis, however, initially showed great interest in figures they could use to demonstrate the incompetence of the Weimar regime.[19]

ECONOMIC STATISTICS AND THE THIRD REICH

When the Nazis assumed power, Wagemann was removed from his post as director of the Reich Statistical Office, owing to internal political intrigue by some of his personal political enemies, but retained his position as director of the IfK. The institute itself was administratively separate from the Reich Statistical Office. In the course of the ensuing push to go down the path to rearmament and war planning, the need for usable figures and empirical data for planning purposes arose. However, the disarray of multiple agencies and decision-making bodies under the Nazis, the coexistence of official authorities, and separate party organs and institutions also had an impact on the field of statistics. No unified institutional statistical body was in charge of compiling data, but the confusing institutional landscape of Nazi Germany was mirrored by a confusing number of institutions compiling statistics.

National income statistics did not play a role either in the Nazis' political rhetoric or in their economic and military decision-making processes. In the German calculation of national income, a distinction was made between the activities of the state that were directly available to end consumers and those that instead were to be seen as intermediate products, production inputs, or costs. Thus, it was necessary to have access to data on government spending to calculate national income. Yet that was becoming ever more difficult.[20] Information on government expenditure was classified as secret, meaning that in 1938 the Reich Statistical Office had to discontinue its regular assessments of national income.[21] Overall, the liberal practice of publishing economic data was increasingly restricted; from this time onward, most statistics were considered classified information.

Nonetheless, it proved possible to finally realize the long-planned industrial census, in 1936. The statisticians had managed to convince the new leaders that the production data still lacking was decisive for the planned armaments drive and that it could be used to calculate the consumption of and need for important raw materials for the war effort.

Because various institutions vied for control over these figures during the Third Reich, the Reich Statistical Office increasingly lost its role as the monopoly government data source. It also suffered from the ambitious personal plans and objectives of several statisticians close to the regime. The Department of Industrial Production Statistics, which serviced Hermann Göring's Raw Materials and Foreign Currency Commission, was separated from the Reich Statistical Office in 1938 and became known as the Reich Office of Military-Economic Planning. Göring, probably the second most powerful man in Germany, after Hitler, was not only head of the German air force and founder of the Gestapo, Germany's extremely brutal secret police, but also had been put in charge of the German economy and rearmament in the years before the war.[22] The new office was to provide the regime with the necessary information for war-planning purposes. It did not serve its purpose, however. Indeed, when evaluating industrial data in tables based not on prices but on quantities, it got truly bogged down and hardly produced any usable results, even if it did term its summaries "overall national economic accounts."[23]

The irrational way that the Nazis pursued their war objectives was reflected in institutional confusion. It enabled neither efficient central planning nor precise knowledge of the individual economic processes. From an economic perspective, the war was planned on an ad hoc basis.[24] The system of economic statistics in Germany was confused and fragmented. An ever-increasing number of military departments compiled their own statistics—often with diverging results.

The confusion regarding who was responsible for data relating to rearmaments meant that companies received piles of questionnaires from various offices, and they increasingly complained that too much time and effort was being wasted on publishing information.[25] A Central Statistical Committee, specially created in 1939 and under Göring's control, now had to approve every survey in an attempt to solve the issue of confused information—but in fact this only added to the red tape.

After the advances on the Eastern Front had come to a standstill and ever-more-serious ammunition shortages had emerged, Hitler commissioned the new head of the Reich Ministry of Armaments and Munitions, Albert Speer, to come up with a more effective planning concept for economic needs. Speer launched the so-called Central Planning Committee. Then, in 1943, the Ministry of Armaments was converted into the Ministry of Armaments and War Production.

The restructuring was intended to facilitate the development of an information system to enable reliable planning. The Reich Ministry of Economics occupied a key position, reflecting the expertise of the IfK, which, after a niche existence of almost ten years, was once again involved in government work. In 1941, the institute had been renamed the German Institute for Economic Research (Deutsches Institut für Wirtschaftsforschung, or DIW). Classical economic research no longer seemed opportune—Nazi policies had promised an end to economic fluctuations in the markets. The term "business cycle" had become politically charged.[26] The institute became the most important source of data for planning the war economy.

Within the institute—and as part of the story of how national income accounting ultimately came to Germany—the statistician Rolf Wagenführ played a decisive role. He had been working at IfK since the 1920s and now headed the industrial economy research department at DIW.[27] Hans Kehrl, head of the Raw Materials Office at the Ministry of Armaments, as of 1943, saw to it that Wagenführ's department, which collected vital information about industrial production, worked only for his ministry. Kehrl tasked Wagenführ with creating a central department for planning statistics at the ministry's planning office. Until then, armaments of the German Reich had not been effectively documented in statistical terms. Wagenführ was now to collect "everything that can be quantified in numbers" and to coordinate with specialists in the various armament departments and organizations. Cooperation went very smoothly, especially because many of the statisticians Wagenführ consulted had previously worked at the Reich Statistical Office or DIW and were "obsessed with their work."[28] Wagenführ gradually became the central figure in armament statistics. In the final months of the war, he was deputy head of the institute.

The desire for a precise basis for planning assumed such extreme forms that, on Kehrl's instructions, an attempt was made to print the material flows on large tabular diagrams and present them in a single room, in the form of triptych-like altarpieces. In addition to information on selected industries, the office's "main cabinet" was to contain the aggregate data on the overall economy, as well as information on national income. The data was to be produced and analyzed by the institute.

Rarely has the goal of centralizing information and painting an overall picture of the economy taken such extreme forms. The idea here was to physically realize the image of the bird's-eye view of the economy, which Milton Gilbert had used to calculate gross national product. As Tooze notes, the concentration of data in one space and in a single medium—the panels of the "altar"—was also a symbol of power.

Yet, the totalitarian vision was as far as it got. For although in 1943 the room actually existed in which all this information was to be displayed, the information itself did not. Indeed, the available data was fragmentary, disparate, and of little use for planning purposes.[29]

After the Ministry of Economics was hit during a bombing raid and a great many important documents were lost, the institute practically had an information monopoly on issues regarding the overall economy. The remainder of the Reich Statistical Office now conducted only routine tasks.[30]

HOW GROSS NATIONAL PRODUCT CAME TO GERMANY

Shortly before the end of the war, the United States Air Force commissioned an inquiry into the exact consequences of Allied air raids on Germany and whether these raids had been a successful military tool. All that was known about the effects of area bombardment came from the eyewitness reports of the bomber crews and information from reconnaissance flights. These sources did not provide a basis for precise assessments. Thus, in 1944, the United States Strategic Bombing Survey was initiated to independently document the consequences of the destruction as precisely as possible.

Economist John Kenneth Galbraith was tasked with statistically recording the war mobilization effort of the German economy, and its destruction. He had taught at Harvard, was a friend of Milton and Richard Gilbert, and, like them, was a staunch Keynesian. Until 1943, he had had a managerial role at the Office of Price Administration, among the most important tasks of which was analyzing the data of gross national product estimates. Galbraith was so intimately familiar with the method of gross national product calculation, he wrote, that it became part of his "bloodstream," as of 1942 at the latest.[31]

The team supporting him included several illustrious figures, and many of Galbraith's staff went on to make a name for themselves. Hungarian-born Nicholas Kaldor, for example, later became a world-famous economist at Cambridge. Tibor Scitovsky, likewise from Hungary, was to criticize American society's focus on growth and consumerism in *The Joyless Economy*, published in the 1970s. Ernst Friedrich Schumacher was a German émigré whose book *Small Is Beautiful*, published in the same year as Scitovsky's, was to become a bible of the antigrowth movement. Another staff member, Russian-born Paul Baran, arguably the best-known American neo-Marxist of the postwar era (and surely, as Galbraith noted, the only one with a tenured professorship), also published a classic work of growth-critical literature, *The Political Economy of Growth*, in 1957. Edward Denison was also a member and, alongside Milton Gilbert, was another protagonist of American gross national product calculation.[32]

Galbraith organized his "economics faculty," as he jokingly called his team, according to different sectors of the economy, orienting himself on the sector classification of the American method of calculating gross national product. First, production data was to be ascertained for each economic sector of the German Reich. Then the influence of the bombings was to be calculated, both on total product and, subsequently, broken down into individual sectors and key industries.

In the final weeks of the war, the members of Galbraith's group were assigned to Allied units fighting in Germany. They were to gather numbers on the ground and to find out which institutions and decision makers absolutely needed to be questioned. It quickly transpired that an overall picture of the German economy was needed, and this being the case, the group was dependent on the knowledge of experts who were able to interpret the available figures and statistics.

Galbraith interrogated Hermann Göring and Albert Speer; in May 1945, Scitovsky and Kaldor interviewed Karl-Otto Saur, who had been state secretary in Speer's ministry. Saur told them that there were important documents on armaments production, located in Leipzig. Shortly before the Red Army took control of the city, Scitovsky and Kaldor managed to secure the documents.[33]

Galbraith's team set up its headquarters in Bad Nauheim, outside Frankfurt, where parts of the Reich Statistical Office—particularly the statistics on machinery—had been evacuated during the war.[34] One person who was obviously to prove indispensable for the success of Galbraith's work was Rolf Wagenführ.

Wagenführ was one of the few public figures who had stayed in Berlin during the last phases of the war, and he was won over by the Soviets right after the fighting ended, in May 1945. He was to start keeping statistics on the Soviet zone. Wagenführ was not unknown to the Russians now in command. He had examined Soviet statistics in his first academic publications. Some even considered him a "roast beef Nazi"—brown on the outside, red on the inside.[35] When he found out that the Americans wanted to question him, he quickly moved his place of residence from the Western part of the city to the Soviet sector.

Galbraith set Paul Baran the task of bringing Wagenführ to Bad Nauheim. Baran had studied in Berlin and had then worked in the Soviet Union for several years, before being persecuted there for a "sustained lack of discipline" and being forced to flee. He gathered a small group of men together to accompany him; they went to Berlin, kidnapped Wagenführ from his bed in the night, and flew him to Bad Nauheim.

No one had anticipated how violently the Soviets would react to the kidnapping. Marshal Georgy Zhukov personally appealed to General Dwight D. Eisenhower, who was enraged by the incident. While Galbraith considered how to hand Wagenführ back to the Russians after questioning him, another member of the group pitched in: Jürgen Kuczynski. As a member of the German Communist Party, the Wuppertal-born son of a famous economics statistician had gone to Britain as an exile and was recruited by the Office of Strategic Services, the American intelligence agency, in London. He knew Wagenführ from days they had spent in Berlin together, and he offered to accompany Wagenführ, allegedly because Kuczynski wanted to know whether his own library and his apartment still existed.

The Soviets received the pair in Berlin with open arms.[36] Kuczynski finished his work for Galbraith and then relocated to East Berlin. He embarked on a unique academic career in East Germany and became one of the best-known intellectuals, with a direct influence on the highest political circles. Wagenführ was likewise to set out a stellar career, but on the other side of the iron curtain: he left Berlin and initially was entrusted with conducting the statistics of the British zone. Later, among other things, he headed the statistics department of the European Coal and Steel Community, took up a professorial chair for statistics in Heidelberg, and was the first director of the Statistical Office of the European Communities, today's Eurostat, in Luxembourg. In a commemorative essay in Wagenführ's honor, Kuczynski, who remained in lifelong contact with him, named Wagenführ a "noble knight of statistics."[37] That an East German not only would stay friends with someone as prominent as Wagenführ but also would go as far as to offer this sort of praise was unheard of during the Cold War.

Wagenführ proved to be an incredible source of information for Galbraith.[38] His data supplied the missing pieces of the mosaic, with the help of which Galbraith's team was able to calculate the first estimate of gross national product for Germany.[39] It is not without a certain irony that, later, after the method of gross national product calculation had completed its triumphal universal march, most of the people involved in this calculation became some of its fiercest critics.

Galbraith was surprised by the results of his calculations and surveys because they, for the first time, provided a clear picture of the Nazi economy. Because no set of tools comparable to gross national product calculation existed on the German side, the military leaders had obviously not been in any position to correctly assess the country's productive potential, let alone tap it. Although an immense amount of data had been collected, the key that would have made it into useful information was missing. In methodological terms, the Germans had nothing to set against gross national product. No statistical tool provided the Nazis with a useful overview of their own economic might. In his concluding report, therefore, Galbraith acknowledged that Kuznets and his successors had seemingly contributed just as much to the Allied victory as several infantry divisions together.[40]

THE GERMAN GROSS NATIONAL PRODUCT CALCULATION

Under the framework of the Marshall Plan (the European Recovery Program), West Germany had to produce an estimate of gross national product. Although Ferdinand Grünig had compiled his own national accounts while working at DIW in 1947, these calculations were methodologically different. The Americans' crucial requirement was that the figure of gross national product now had to be given as an *official* figure—not as the estimate of a research institute. Only a public institution could do that, even if, as yet, Germany had no functioning government.

Thus, gross national product and its method of calculation were introduced in Germany by means of outside pressure and as a sovereign task from the outset. After the war, however, official statistics in Germany had to be painstakingly established. Destruction, the division of the country, the establishment of new statistical offices in different occupation zones, missing documents, and a lack of experts worked against efforts to compile coherent statistics. Furthermore, modern methods of calculating gross national product were unknown to German statisticians, who had been cut off from the international debates revolving around calculating national income; indeed, such calculations had been unimportant during the Nazi period. The introduction of national accounts was a "catch-up modernization."[41]

In January 1948 (more than one year before the Federal Republic of Germany was created), the statistical office of the so-called United Economic Territory was founded in Wiesbaden for the British–American Bizone, which had been established one year before.[42] This office was now given the task of calculating gross national product in order to fulfill the requirements of the Marshall Plan.[43] External expertise was needed for this, however. To this end, the National Accounts Research Unit, headed by Richard Stone, was founded in Cambridge in 1949.

A problem emerged when staff at the statistical office set about conducting the calculations. The Reich Statistical Office had compiled its assessment of national income solely using tax statistics. In order to use the new method to calculate gross national product from the production side for 1948, it was necessary to take the findings of the 1936 industrial census as the basis and then update them. The statisticians could not wait for more recent data, which they themselves would have had to gather.[44]

The data from the industrial census was located on Klosterstrasse, in Berlin's Mitte district, where the Department of Industrial Production Statistics had been based until the end of the war; after the main building of the Reich Statistical Office was damaged, its documents had been taken to Klosterstrasse. Thus, following the division of Berlin, these documents were located in the Soviet sector and were not freely accessible.[45] "They were sitting on the documents and we couldn't get to them," recalled the later head of the Federal Statistical Office, Hildegard Bartels. At a loss, the statisticians reported the dilemma to the American control officer of the office, who was considered particularly reckless and did not hesitate long. His idea was to go in and simply grab the documents. Former Reich Statistical Office staff described to him precisely where the industrial census documents could be found in the building on Klosterstrasse. The officer broke in and "snatched everything he could get his hands on," said Bartels. "He was very proud of it and we were exceedingly grateful to him."[46]

Whereas, for their initial calculation of German gross national product, the Americans had been reliant on kidnapping people, for the first official German estimate it was sufficient to steal documents. The calculations based on them were published in 1949 in the journal *Wirtschaft und Statistik*, issued by the statistical office. They had been made "by the [European Recovery Program] working group National Economic Accounts," which included "the Statistical Office of the United Economic Territory, the business and financial administrations, and the Bank deutscher Länder." The key sentence in this first report was succinct: "The calculation methods have been adjusted to those conventionally used in Anglo-Saxon countries."[47] The American–British method began its triumphal onward march around the globe.

The exact meaning of "national product" first had to be clarified in Germany: "By calculating national income and national product one seeks an overall expression of a country's economic performance, a figure for the results of economic activity and the annual supply of goods and conveniences of life to a population. National income or net national product refer to the entirety of goods and services valued in money that are available to an economy annually for consumption and investment after preserving the initial wealth status."[48]

The new figures saw their first practical application in the calculation of the real income of certain social strata in relation to social product. This calculation was conducted for the first time in 1949, for "industrial workers," and was likewise published in an article in *Wirtschaft und Statistik*. Recalling the major internal political tensions that studies on income distribution had caused, particularly in the Weimar Republic, the statistical office described this calculation as "delicate": "The Office requests that this article be taken for what it is, namely an attempt to give an idea of the most important orders of magnitude. There is no valuation connected to this. It is not the statistician's job to judge whether development hitherto was socially desirable or not, whether it can be seen as economically expedient or not."[49]

Initially, however, the German political scene showed little interest in the figures. The positive, practical experiences this system had given rise to in the United States were lacking here. The old rifts between economists over the sense of such a number system even flared up again and continued until well into the 1950s. Heidelberg-based economist

Werner Hofmann wrote that the figures were "national economic miniature paintings." He claimed that the, by definition, balanced accounts painted a picture of "perfect harmony" that had little to do with the real circumstances and only existed in planned economies.[50]

The political world, particularly economics minister Ludwig Erhard, also initially linked the national accounts with planning and planned economies and viewed the data with great skepticism.[51] In France, in contrast, politicians immediately recognized the benefit of the number system. It could be used not only to help that country plan its economic reconstruction but also, it was hoped, to find its way back to international standing and prevent such a humiliation as its quick defeat in 1940 from happening again in the future. The French considered the national accounts to be "accounts of power."[52]

German reservations quickly disappeared, however, as the accounts proved to be a versatile information tool that could be used to define economic aggregates, which were important for politics. The Ministry of Finance, for example, was interested in the level of the national product, because the payments for the planned (and later rejected) European Defence Community were to be calculated with reference to it. Moreover, it emerged that the statistics could be used as a basis for tax estimates, the budget, and medium-term financial planning.[53] As economic growth started to pick up, politicians' skepticism evaporated entirely. Gross national product finally became the most powerful political number, and political arithmetic won out in Germany, too—the country that originally had been defeated by it.

6

THE ULTIMATE TRIUMPH OF GROSS NATIONAL PRODUCT

In the political sphere of the United States, gross national product was a concept with positive connotations. It was directly associated with military victory in World War II. The dramatic increase in military spending in 1942 had been part of President Roosevelt's so-called Victory Program. The American military strategy during the war envisaged bringing opponents to their knees by producing massive amounts of armaments, and gross national product statistically demonstrated the transformation achieved by the American economy and the military successes. As historian Russell Weigley put it in his book *The American Way of War*, World War II was a "gross national product war."[1] Gross national product stood not only for economic but also for military and political success. Immediately after the war, it was to prove itself anew.

The U.S. administration was aware, even before the end of the war, that the return to a peacetime economy would once again signify a fundamental economic change. Roosevelt had made it clear that statistical information would be indispensable in this. Milton Gilbert and the Department of Commerce helped ensure that the notion of gross national product won the day in peacetime too.[2]

Shortly after the end of the war, the necessity to expand production and raise gross national product was generally recognized by politicians. The United States was gripped with the fear that uncontrollable mass unemployment— similar to that seen during the Great Depression—might occur again. Politicians sought to prevent this at all cost. Adding to this were fears of stagnation that had been floating around people's heads since the late nineteenth century, when John Stuart Mill had described how the economy would stop expanding as soon as the final stage of industrial development had been reached. Against the background of the experiences of the Great Depression, what Mill saw as a matter-of-fact law became a nightmare scenario. In addition, Keynesian theory permitted the assumption that stagnation and accompanying chronic unemployment could become permanent.[3] Above all, however, it was the academic world that adhered to Keynes's theory; it was largely disputed among industrialists and businesspeople, and it was widely rejected by them and by many politicians.[4]

But now it seemed that increasing gross national product would avert economic disaster. As long as it was possible to increase production output, there was no danger of economic stagnation.[5] With the Employment Act of 1946, the expansion of production became a government objective; only in this way could full employment be achieved. Whereas during the war years one could see from the gross national product statistics how armaments production increased, during peacetime the growth in the production of consumer and capital goods showed that it was possible to create more jobs. Given that combating unemployment equated to nothing less than maintaining social coherence, gross national product was also able to serve as a measure of the internal political and social stability of a country.

Under these new conditions, gross national product garnered special political attention. The system of national accounts also contained important statistical information, of course, but it was gross national product itself that became the all-important figure, the numerical metaphor for the state of the economy and, as such, for the state of a country—the figure without which it was impossible to imagine political discussion.

The belief that an expansion of production such as had been seen during wartime would be possible going forward, and would thus guarantee employment and prosperity, corresponded with a historic change of mind-set within the political establishment of the United States. Future prospects were no longer shaped by fear and pessimism but by the idea of an increasingly possible improvement through growth.

Archetypal in this context was the 1945 book *The Bogey of Economic Maturity*, by George Terborgh, who sought to refute the hypothesis of inevitable economic stagnation, and Chester Bowles's 1946 book *Tomorrow Without Fear*, in which Bowles clearly described the expansion of production as the key to the future felicity of American society. Bowles claimed that people could safely bid farewell to the opinion, still prevalent during the New Deal, that not all structural and social problems could be solved by economic policy. Yet he was less interested in expansion, in the sense of a better use of idle productive capacities, than in the concept of economic growth, still mostly unknown at the time.[6]

In the context of the Employment Act, the Council of Economic Advisers also was set up. This novel advisory body of the U.S. president started work in 1946. Only a few of its members were economists who worked purely in an academic field; most had experience in politics or in industry and thus in the private sector. They were open to Keynesian ideas but didn't follow them blindly.

The council established and consolidated the political dogma of the necessity of economic expansion and growth. It became a vehement advocate of what was later to be termed "growthmanship": the idea that increasing gross national product must be accorded absolute political priority. Growth was the decisive factor in politics—more important than distribution of wealth or other social parameters—and would solve America's material and social problems. Consequently, politics was "the politics of productivity."[7]

This approach was different from the old political approaches of the New Deal or Keynesianism, and was one with no clear theoretical basis, because the idea of growth had no place in the economic theories of the day. Economists did not turn their attention to it until several years later. The council advisers derived their political recommendations from the experiences of wartime and the immediate postwar period and based their opinions on gross national product statistics. The knowledge these statistics supplied "stood above all others in significance" in their advice about economic policy.[8]

In its publications and statements, the council repeatedly referenced gross national product statistics and, in so doing, ensured the concept's ongoing spread within the political domain. In *Nation's Economic Budget*, regularly released from 1947 onward, the council presented a condensed version of the national accounts based on the new Department of Commerce system. They used it to show not only the composition of the aggregated national product but also (among other things) how much of its creation and use was attributable to private households, companies, foreign trade, and the state. In 1948, a reviewer for the *New York Times* euphorically wrote of these figures, "This is not somebody's crackbrained theory; it is simple arithmetic."[9] The ideas of William Petty and Colin Clark, of a politics founded on empirical evidence, seemed to have been realized in textbook fashion. Arithmetic came before theory and had significant political relevance.

INTERNATIONAL HARMONIZATION

The concept of gross national product was becoming increasingly important internationally as well. The Marshall Plan played a special role here. The European Recovery Act, which formed the legal basis for the plan, provided for the establishment of the Economic Cooperation Administration (ECA), which would coordinate aid payments. It was headed by Paul Hoffman, the former president of the Studebaker automobile company.

In 1942, Hoffman had founded the Committee for Economic Development, a think tank where academics and businesspeople set out to solve the economic problems of both wartime and the postwar period. He vehemently championed the idea that increases in growth and productivity would lead to a peacetime economy of material abundance. During the war, Studebaker had produced aircraft engines and military trucks in addition to automobiles, so Hoffman was well aware of the effects of the wartime economy and the expansion of production. In his view, the future of Europe likewise lay in an expansion of production. He shared the view that was swiftly taking root in American politics; namely, that the dogma of growth had to be applied globally, and especially in defeated Germany. For some time during and shortly after the war, opponents of this view had tried to enforce a cap on industrial expansion for postwar Germany, though ultimately without success.[10]

The ECA faced a mammoth task. It had to assess the economic situation of very different Western European economies, calculate the funds needed for reconstruction, and evaluate the consequences such assistance would have. Given that the Americans had used gross national product calculations during the war to assess not only their own economic power and defense capabilities but also that of other countries, it was only a small step to requesting corresponding figures and national accounts from beneficiary countries to aid the ECA's centralized coordination of reconstruction assistance.[11]

At the instigation of the ECA, along with the National Accounts Research Unit in Cambridge, headed by Richard Stone, the Organisation for European Economic Cooperation (OEEC) was founded in Paris.[12] The group's primary task, in addition to distributing assistance payments, was to ensure the comparability of statistical information. Stone's job was to develop a simplified, standardized system of national accounts for the OEEC, along with training programs to familiarize staff at the statistical authorities with the calculations.

Milton Gilbert likewise played an important role in this context. Close friends with Stone since their 1944 meeting, he headed the Economics and Statistics department at the OEEC from 1950 until 1961 and was in charge of the national accounts there.[13] In 1952, the OEEC published the Standardised System of National Accounts, which formed the basis of the United Nations System of National Accounts, which was repeatedly adjusted and, to this day, is considered the standard document for the international harmonization of calculations.[14]

Some countries (such as the Netherlands, France, and Norway) developed their own systems, and in the United States, too, the accounts and calculation logic used from 1947 (the national income and product accounts) differed somewhat from those used in Great Britain, where Meade's and Stone's method was readjusted in the early 1950s. Even so, the variances were only in the details; fundamentally, the methods were the same. This was particularly true of the orientation on production and therefore on gross national product, which consequently displaced the older concept of national income as the most important political figure.

Yet the Marshall Plan did not simply finance the reconstruction of Europe and supply the appropriate statistical calculation tool for it. The Marshall Plan propagated a vision. Looking back, Paul Hoffman wrote, " 'You Too Can Be Like

Us': that was the original message of the Marshall Plan, and it was the task of the Information Programme to bring it home to Europeans everywhere. They learned that this is the land of full shelves and bulging shops, made possible by high productivity and good wages, and that its prosperity may be emulated elsewhere by those who will work towards it."[15]

Gross national product (both absolute and as a per capita indicator) supplied the necessary yardstick for this vision. It enabled a comparison between states and had simultaneously become an important target: people wanted to reach the level that was found in the United States. The ideal scenario was considered to be a convergence: the gradual alignment of economies that had developed differently and the economy of the United States. The Enlightenment model of progress had shaped large parts of the nineteenth century, as well as colonialism, and had assumed that the world's different societies would increasingly adjust to the socially and culturally superior Western nations, in the course of the linear process of civilization. This model was now obsolete. In the new convergence model, the social and cultural dimension came second. The initial concern was with the economy and was geared to ostensibly objective and neutral figures: The idea of catch-up development hinged on a harmonization of gross national product.

THE ECONOMIC THEORY OF GROWTH

The focus on growth of gross national product enabled the linkage of domestic challenges to promote employment with the vision of international convergence and the expectation of increasing economic and political strength. The role of gross national product or GDP as a political phenomenon is inextricably linked to the idea of growth. However, modern economic theories of growth did not emerge until after the idea of its necessity had already gained a sure footing in American politics.

Although classical economic theory had traditionally propagated the expansion of production, by dint of being oriented on a materially founded concept of growth, the subsequent neoclassical theory had concerned itself more with the shaping of the laws of the self-balancing market, not with the dynamic processes of growth and expansion. Moreover, economic research, which had reached its peak in the interwar period, concentrated on looking for laws that would explain the short-term ups and downs of the business cycle. When it emerged, Keynesian theory was geared to the underemployment equilibrium evident during the Great Depression and was likewise initially unsuitable as a long-term growth strategy. Keynes himself criticized the American belief in sustainable growth by means of the expansion of production, shortly before his death in 1946.

In order to ensure it had common ground with modern growth theory, Keynesian theory first had to be made more dynamic and linked to the idea of increasing gross national product (this will be touched upon further, below). Colin Clark had already attributed great significance to the growth of national income. He not only had compared the economic power of different countries, using per capita income, but also had investigated which conditions needed to be met to enable maximum economic progress for the maximum number of people. It was clear to him that, in many parts of the world, production needed to be increased. For Clark, a future of material abundance was still a long way off. Yet the firm empiricist could not and did not want to substantiate a growth theory of his own with his work.

During the war, some economists had addressed the problem of individual countries' differing economic power. Austrian Paul Rosenstein-Rodan researched this topic in particular. Born in Krakow, he later immigrated to England. In an article published in 1943, he considered how the differences in development between Eastern and Western Europe and between Europe and Asia could be balanced out. His ideal solution was increased industrialization in the context of an international division of labor. Where states were unable to initiate such industrialization themselves, foreign capital assistance should do it for them. Rosenstein-Rodan based his ideas on two assumptions. First, he assumed that there was a great surplus of labor in these countries, which could be absorbed by the growing industrial sector. Second, he thought that the state could and should plan massive industrialization programs.[16]

In 1944, Rosenstein-Rodan gave his ideas greater depth. In an article on the development of "economically backward" regions of the world, he adopted Clark's idea that real per capita income was the only relevant yardstick for progress. He likewise used Clark's data on international income development to show that, during previous decades, it had only been positive in a small part of the world. The countries excluded from growth were getting increasingly impatient, he claimed, as they were not seeing any evidence of progress. Their progress should be directly promoted, he concluded. If only to avoid future conflicts, income and affluence in these countries needed to be boosted. Yet he considered international capital assistance indispensable in order that, as he put it, "they can grow richer 'on their own.' "[17] Investment, so the theory went, would generate growth, and growth in turn would generate employment and political stability, both domestic and international.

The concept of growth underwent a fundamental theoretical innovation with the Keynesian growth theories, strongly stimulated by the work done by Roy Harrod and Evsey Domar. As early as 1939, Harrod had described the conditions for continual growth in his article "An Essay in Dynamic Theory" (though it was barely acknowledged at the time), and he predicted that the shift of focus onto the growth rate would lead to a "mental revolution."[18] Domar addressed the topic in 1946, making a direct reference to national income: "One does not have to be a Keynesian to believe that employment is somehow dependent on national income, and that national income has something to do with investment. But as soon as investment comes in, growth cannot be left out."[19] Investment, according to Domar, could increase both growth and income. Yet, for Domar, growth was not yet a political end in itself. The objective of growth was full employment.[20]

The two writers' essays sparked further speculation on the growth rate, its determinants, and possible ways of influencing it, and thus the optimistic belief emerged that quantitatively defined growth rates could be generated by corresponding investment. Within this logic, growth was primarily a function of investment and thus could be controlled by expanding the production potential of goods (and services). This further reinforced the production focus of the war and postwar years—which also seemed absolutely plausible, given the obvious need for investment and capital in Europe's destroyed cities.

From the 1950s onward, this way of reasoning had a decisive influence on the nascent field of development economics and policy. One assumed that, precisely in the countries then considered part of the Third World, growth processes could be initiated from the outside, through large-scale infrastructure and corresponding industrial projects. In this way, the positive experiences with the Marshall Plan were simply transposed onto the rest of the world. It is no coincidence that several employees of the Economic Cooperation Administration became important development theorists.

Moreover, several of the first growth theorists actively helped gross national product prevail as a definition of development and progress, even within the United Nations system. Particularly noteworthy here is economist and later Nobel laureate Arthur Lewis, who drafted several of the United Nations' early foundation documents on questions of development and, in his 1955 book *The Theory of Economic Growth*, sought to address this topic in depth, in relation to economic theory, for the first time since John Stuart Mill's *Principles of Political Economy* (1848). For Lewis, growth—defined as the rate of change in per capita gross national product—was tantamount to progress and development.[21]

Full employment was not the only goal linked to an increase in gross national product. Chapter IX of the United Nations Charter of 1945 had stipulated that full employment and a higher standard of living should be pursued as common goals of all nations. Economic growth would necessarily raise employment and this, in turn, would lead to an improvement in material living conditions.[22]

The founding document of the Organisation for Economic Co-operation and Development (OECD), which superseded the OEEC in 1960, states that the organization's task is "to achieve the highest sustainable economic growth and employment and a rising standard of living."[23] The trinity of raising gross national product, lowering unemployment, and improving material well-being was the Western credo of the day, and a rising gross national product was considered a visible sign that the two other goals also could be achieved.

GROWTH IN COMPETING SYSTEMS

As early as 1949, Harold G. Moulton, president of the Brookings Institution, considered rising gross national product important, not only because there were still too many families living in material hardship, even in the United States, but also because it was an expression of military power and was "regarded essential to prestige in the family of nations."[24] Growth and the associated material well-being was a key differentiating factor in international comparisons, particularly with the Soviet Union.

Simon Kuznets didn't see the search for full employment or the development challenges of Europe and the Third World as the most important reasons for the universal political success of the dogma of growth. For him, competition with the Soviet Union and the Cold War were decisive. Soviet communism promised an end to social deprivation. What was important was to supply society with the necessary goods and to achieve a previously unknown level of comprehensive material well-being. Material provision, Kuznets claimed, was the "secular religion" of communism.[25] In terms of underlying materialistic thrust, capitalism and communism pursued the same goal, but the paths to get there were different. The competition was to show which system was better suited to satisfying the material needs of the population.

Against the background of the political and economic collapse of the Soviet system in 1989, and the associated triumph of the Western capitalist, liberal economic model as, allegedly, the only functioning and universal path to prosperity, it is hard to imagine just how strongly people doubted their own performance capacity, particularly in the United States, into the 1960s. Indeed, the emergence of the Soviet Union as a nuclear power sparked the beginning not only of an arms race but also of a competition for global economic supremacy. An article published in *Foreign Affairs* magazine in 1953 warned of the Soviet system prevailing, which could result from a potentially higher growth rate there. It was clear what this would mean: "The solution for the problem raised here lies without doubt in the economic field. We must raise our production, and keep the gap between us and them as great as it is now. Otherwise time is on their side."[26]

With the Soviets' first successes in space travel, such as the Sputnik satellite and placing the first human in space, the fear of the Soviet Union's economic and technological growth became ever greater, especially as the Soviet leadership stalwartly insisted that the industry under its control was growing faster than that of the West and would soon overtake it. Because there were no precise figures available, the West did not know how seriously to take this threat. The Americans saw cause for concern. One department of the Central Intelligence Agency was tasked only with calculating a realistic gross national product from Soviet statistics, which would enable a comparison with American economic power.

Development policy, too, established in the 1950s, was shaped by the fear of communism. People were convinced that, if it were possible to ensure constant growth of gross national product in the countries of the Third World, these states would be immune to the promises of communism. As early as 1949, President Truman made it clear that development policy served to defend against communism. The fixation on an increase in per capita income and on the expansion of growth in Third World countries had a strong political component from the very beginning.

The international rivalry was not restricted to the two superpowers, however. The countries of Western Europe also compared among themselves their economic growth and increases in per capita income. In 1954, the OEEC submitted the first comparative study of gross national product calculations based on the standardized method. The United Nations followed suit in 1957, but used the OEEC figures.[27]

The focus on growth reached its climax in the 1960s. By this time, the Keynesian-inspired idea of setting a clear growth rate for gross national product had definitively won the day in the political arena. In the United States, the Democratic presidential candidate, John F. Kennedy, promised to ensure an annual growth rate of 5 percent. Within the OECD, too, target growth was firmly set in figures. Member states pledged to collectively increase their growth by 50 percent during the 1960s.[28] In 1967, the Act to Promote Economic Stability and Growth came into force in Germany. Economic stability was now inconceivable without growth. Indeed, according to the act, economic and finance policy measures needed to correspond to the "requirements of maintaining a macroeconomic balance," and under conditions "of constant and suitable economic growth," at that.

THE BEGINNING OF A NEW ERA

The consequences of the continual rise in gross national product in Western societies quickly surpassed all expectations. What happened in the late 1950s was not just an economic transformation but an unforeseen social sea change, too. John Kenneth Galbraith impressively described this in 1958, in his book *The Affluent Society*. Economics as a discipline had evolved at a time when the majority of people were destitute, and economic theory as well as economic policy could not avoid addressing the problem of mass poverty. Today, however, this topic belonged to the past.[29] The phenomenon of mass poverty, the social question, no longer existed.[30]

Traditionally, the topic of inequality was closely bound up with poverty. Social inequality, in particular inequal income and wealth distribution, had given rise to the call, which had grown ever louder over the course of the nineteenth century, for the propertied classes to give the poorer classes a portion of their wealth. On the other hand, liberal thinkers and politicians argued that inequality was a just and a necessary evil and that those who worked should be able to enjoy the fruits of their labor. The theory common at this time was that redistribution would create the wrong incentives in society and lead to everyone faring worse. Only with the existence of wealth could sufficient funds be pooled and invested to enable the creation of jobs for the poor in the first place. In short, economic progress was not possible without inequality. Adam Smith had made similar arguments.

In the 1950s, however, it seemed the problem had resolved itself. Galbraith wrote, "Few things are more evident in modern social history than the decline of interest in inequality. . . . Inequality has ceased to preoccupy men's minds."[31] Whereas fifty years before, nothing had been discussed more fiercely than how to ensure a fairer distribution of wealth by means of suitable taxes, this was now no longer seen as a political problem. Yet, as Galbraith pointed out, this was not because inequality had decreased but because full employment and rising wages had improved the situation of those on the bottom rungs of society. Consequently, he noted, the call for a redistribution of wealth had faded away—increasing wages had made it irrelevant.

For Galbraith, the historical specificity of the modern world was that an increase in the volume of goods produced directly changed the economic situation of the entire population, including that of the poorer members of society. In the past, the poor had not cared whether more was produced or not, he claimed, as it had no direct impact on their lives. It is not until the individual notices that an increase in production personally benefits him that he has an incentive to contribute to the improvement of his output, his production methods, or technological progress.

As such, the expansion of production in developed economies, and with it the growth of gross national product, was an effective alternative to redistribution. In historical terms, the expansion of production was the cement holding society together. It had neutralized the social tensions once spawned by inequality. Focusing on greater production was the magic formula that fueled the belief, among both the rich and the poorer classes, in the advantages of corresponding policy making. Indeed, striving for a high gross national product was a social consensus, for it benefited everyone.[32]

The continually improving situation of the poorer members of society was borne out by real figures: "It is the increase in output in recent decades, not the redistribution of income, which has brought the great material improvement for the average man."[33] What economic growth was able to achieve was incredible. The historically unparalleled increase in gross national product not only had improved material well-being and put an end to poverty and hardship but also had stifled debate about how much personal ownership was permissible and who had to give a portion to whom. Thus, concentrating on economic growth was a political necessity.

Ludwig Erhard (1897–1977) also described the transformative power of society, which was linked to a rise in gross national product, looking at the example of Germany in his 1957 book *Prosperity Through Competition* (the original title in German was *Wohlstand für Alle*, which would translate as *Prosperity for All*). Erhard was the first minister of economics in West Germany (as of 1949) and one of the most popular German politicians of the immediate postwar period. His popularity was founded, above all, on the surge in economic growth that set in while he was in office, which noticeably helped improve living conditions for many millions of people, after the hardships of the war and the postwar years. This, in a mixture of amazement, pride, and appreciation, was called the "economic miracle."

Erhard himself seemed to embody this development. Of a portly stature, he most liked to have his picture taken holding a fat cigar and was known by the nicknames "The Man with the Cigar" or "Mr. Economic Miracle." He was a gifted orator and made skillful use of the media to promote himself and his policies. So great was his popularity, and so strongly was he connected with the economic successes of West Germany, that in the 1960s Erhard even became the second federal chancellor of West Germany, after Adenauer. He acted somewhat haplessly in this function, however, and was ousted from office after just three years. Yet, what was particularly noteworthy about Erhard was not his economic policies but his book. *Prosperity Through Competition* can be seen almost as Erhard's (and early West Germany's) economic policy creed. It was an instant best seller and was translated into more than a dozen languages (it came out in America in 1958). The work is still in print to this day.

It was rare for a German politician to be able to reach such a broad public with a book, let alone a book about the economy and economic policy. Coming out at almost the exact same time as Galbraith's, Erhard's book had a different significance, given the perception of him in Germany. While Galbraith was perceived as an academic and Harvard professor, Erhard, although an economics professor, was, in the eyes of the Germans, above all a politician. As such, his arguments show more strongly than Galbraith's how politics addressed and instrumentalized the topic of growth and raising productivity. *Prosperity Through Competition* is therefore an extremely important contemporary document that, owing to its enormous diffusion in other Western countries, has no real equivalent and is particularly suitable for understanding how the belief in growth became politically manifest.

According to Erhard, before World War II, only a small upper class had been able to achieve a high material standard of living. For this reason, he stated, economic policy had, above all, to create the necessary conditions "to lead ever widening circles of the German people towards prosperity." People needed to "overcome the old conservative social structure once and for all," as well as the "ill-feeling between rich and poor."[34]

The basic idea was, rather, "to increase prosperity by expansion than to try for a different distribution of the national income by pointless quarrelling." And the figures Erhard was able to present spoke for themselves. The first table in the book shows the development of German national product from 1936 to 1956—it had doubled between 1949 and the time the book was published. Erhard notes, "This measure of the undisputed success of the policy demonstrates how much more sensible it is to concentrate all available energies on increasing the nation's wealth rather than to squabble over the distribution of this wealth, and thus be side-tracked from the fruitful path of increasing gross national product. It is considerably easier to allow everyone a larger slice out of a bigger cake than to gain anything by discussing the division of a smaller cake."[35]

Moreover, during this time, private consumption had increased more strongly in Germany than in any other OEEC country. "Even the most revolutionary reform of our social order could never have provoked such an increase, or part of it, in the private consumption of this or that group compared to what was in fact achieved. Any such attempt would have led to the paralysis and stagnation of our economy." Anyone, however, who reflected on a more just distribution of gross national product (Erhard put the word *just* in quotes) was a clear advocate of the despicable ideology of seeking to "gain advantages at the expense of others."[36]

Germany had seen full employment since 1954, which Erhard had considered to be "the most desirable aim," given the country's experience of crisis in the 1930s. For him, the endless pursuit of material goods virtually guaranteed progress and civilization. Although the goods Erhard had in mind were very modest from today's point of view—refrigerators, washing machines, vacuum cleaners, perhaps even a car—the ever-increasing consumption would, he wrote, bring about nothing less than the "happy and healthy development" of the world.[37]

Consequently, the increase in standard of living he sought was "concerned less with the problems of division than with problems of production and productivity." The solution was to be found in "multiplying the national income [i.e., gross national product]." Erhard continued, "Egyptian pyramids were not built for their own sake; no, every new machine, each new power station, every new factory and any other means whereby productivity can be increased, serve in the final instance to enrich all who live and work within the sphere of the social market economy. I shall never tire of ensuring that the fruits of economic progress will benefit ever widening circles of the population and finally everyone."[38]

The historically unprecedented objective of raising gross national product was to achieve prosperity for all. This objective could only be formulated in this way, however, because the old way of thinking of business cycles as an "irrefutable" law, with incalculable social consequences, had lost its validity. Since the late 1940s, it had seemed that the eternal ups and downs of the economic rhythm had been overcome, and full employment and continual economic advancement had become the new law. Increasing gross national product was the perfect path to happiness.

Galbraith and Erhard reflected traditional economic positions in their observations. Adam Smith's idea of "universal opulence" based on ever-greater productivity and ever-expanding production finally seemed to have become reality. Without wishing to elaborate on the father of modern economics, both authors precisely described the scenario Smith had presented in his magnum opus *The Wealth of Nations*. They also outlined the solution to social hardship through material well-being and increased production, as had been propagated by Alfred Marshall and Arthur Pigou. Now, however, a general, theoretical, basic assumption had become an observable mechanism that could be steered. It seemed the increase in goods production, a necessity in sociopolitical terms, was bearing fruit.

Erhard also had an answer to the question of whether the focus on ever-greater growth would not lead to a "soulless materialism": paradoxically, greater prosperity was able to liberate man "from a purely primitive materialistic way of thinking." For, as long as people are "overwhelmed with the grievances of everyday life," it is hardly surprising that they strive for "material considerations." Prosperity on the other hand would lead to people being "conscious of their own worth, their personality and their human dignity," enabling them to "[free] themselves from materialistic thinking."[39] A society must, he said, strive for growth in order to also enable those of its members whose social standard was still unsatisfactory to benefit from such spiritual and cultural development: "Those sectors which now enjoy higher consumption more and more must not be criticized, since, first of all, the goods they are now able to purchase represent the fulfilment of a long-felt want, or because they are not yet able to place spiritual, cultural and material values in their proper order in satisfying their wants. With greater security of social well-being the stage will surely be reached when the differences between the good and the bad, and what is valuable and what is not, will be more clearly recognized."[40]

Material well-being was not an end in itself, but a means to an end. Ultimately, people wanted "better results . . . than merely a larger number of beefsteaks and cutlets."[41] The aim was to encourage people to reevaluate their lifestyles. Yet, ultimately, that was not the task of an economic policy maker. In any case, the day would come, Erhard noted, when people would no longer see salvation in increasing material well-being.

For Ludwig Erhard there was still a long way to go. After all, he also had no doubt that German gross national product and, with it, material living standards would initially have to conform to the American model.

CONCLUSION

Although the necessity of raising gross national product seemed to become an established goal in the global political arena in the 1960s, pushback soon began. It was not just the focus on rising material affluence and the increasingly apparent negative social and ecological consequences of increased production that provoked social criticism. Indeed, gross national product itself and its methodology of calculation were subjected to scrutiny.[1] When the "grievances of everyday life" in most Western nations had been overcome, and historically high levels of material standards of living had been reached, criticism of the dominance of the materialist concept of growth also emerged. The meaningfulness of what Walt Rostow termed the "age of high mass consumption," based on the American "way of life," and which was seen by him as the pinnacle of civilization, was increasingly questioned.[2]

It seemed that what Ludwig Erhard had predicted was coming to pass: the move away from a "materialistic thinking." The critique of gross national product and of the idea of unlimited growth has gained momentum ever since, and the critics have certainly not fallen silent.[3] In recent years, this dialogue has triggered a number of political initiatives that search for alternative welfare measures to supplement gross domestic product and growth statistics.

The Istanbul Declaration, drafted in 2007 by the World Bank, the Organisation for Economic Co-operation and Development, the European Commission, and the United Nations Development Programme (among others), was one of the first international documents to call for wider and improved measurements of social progress to supplement GDP. In a major international conference hosted by the European Parliament, the Club of Rome, and the OECD in the same year, the issue was debated under the heading "Beyond GDP." This later became the Beyond GDP initiative of the European Commission. The starting point of all these initiatives was the observation that GDP and growth were no longer adequate indicators of welfare and that they misrepresented what citizens really value.

In 2008, French president Nicolas Sarkozy set up a high-ranking, expert Commission on the Measurement of Economic Performance and Social Progress, led by a number of eminent economists, including Joseph Stiglitz and Amartya Sen. Their proposals as to what indicators could be used to supplement the dominant focus on growth, expressed in their final report, in 2009, have had a lasting influence on subsequent international debates.

Various countries have taken up the challenge to search for and define alternative welfare indicators; among these are Canada and Australia, but also Italy, the United States, and the United Kingdom. In Germany, a parliamentary expert commission was set up in 2010 with two main objectives: to search for alternative welfare indicators and to discuss the role that economic growth still plays within Germany's political culture. On this second issue, the commission was strongly divided and reached no consensus. The final report of 2013 thus contained two different chapters on the issue of growth. One argued for the need to "dethrone" GDP growth and look for alternative strategies; the other advocated the need to continue with the traditional focus on growth.[4]

The German case is symptomatic in that although it was dissatisfaction with the dominance of growth that led to the search for alternative welfare indicators in the first place, international organizations and national governments have not dismissed the importance of growth and GDP. However, it is often acknowledged that growth somehow has to be modern or "qualitative" in order to be justifiable. In the wording of the European Commission's 2020 Strategy, growth should be "smart," "sustainable" and "inclusive." The EU initiative Beyond GDP was later renamed GDP and Beyond, making it clear that there was no intention of abandoning growth and GDP altogether.

Seemingly, national politicians who embrace the idea of alternative welfare measures feel the need to reassure parts of their constituencies that growth is still of major importance. British prime minister David Cameron, who initiated a large-scale national debate on progress and welfare, stated in his "Speech on Wellbeing" (2010), "First and foremost, people are concerned that talking about wellbeing shows that this government is somehow sidelining economic growth as our first concern. . . . Now, let me be very, very clear: growth is the essential foundation of all our aspirations."[5]

In other words, little has changed in terms of the central role that both gross national product (called GDP since the 1990s) and growth continue to play in our political culture. Not only is GDP still considered the most important "indicator for analyzing an economy's economic performance and welfare development," but as an international benchmark, too, GDP is more important than ever. "GDP has survived all attacks on its right to exist to date," as German economist Rolf Kroker put it, for it has enduringly proved its political usefulness.[6]

William Petty had envisaged precisely such a development. His ideas on political arithmetic became reality with the triumph of gross national product and GDP. Petty dreamed that politics one day would be based on figures, on an empirical system that would explain the "perplexed and intricate ways of the World," convey the power and fame of the monarch, and help improve humankind's fortunes. In his day, this still seemed pure fantasy.

Interest in statistics on national income did not arise until the middle of the Great Depression, and this can be attributed to the fact that, for a long time, people were not able to understand the "perplexed and intricate ways" of the economy. However, national income was not yet a suitable basis for the development of a complete political arithmetic. Although Colin Clark had performed pioneering work with his methodological reflections on the assessment of national income and on the usefulness of international comparison, as well as with initial theoretical reflections on recording and measuring economic growth, his ideas still did not turn into a modern political arithmetic as he had hoped.

Simon Kuznets, in contrast, plays the role of the anti-Petty in the history of GDP. His reflections and calculations on national income were far too cautious to serve as a useful tool for a government. It wasn't until his former students at the Department of Commerce used Keynesian theory to modify his ideas on the statistical recording of economic processes, and until political attention shifted from income to the volume of goods produced (owing to the necessity to adapt the economy to the requirements of war, and thus to fundamentally transform it) that the attempt to use figures to understand the economy truly became political arithmetic— a number system that was defined by the state, served the state's interests, and documented and therefore legitimated government actions.

With the triumph of gross national product and the accompanying shift in focus to production, a statistics with merely historical value (as the first analyses of national income were an attempt to come to grips with what had happened in the past) suddenly became a tool for forecasting the future and for government planning in the present. Gross national product had proved its worth during war planning, and after the war, too, people saw in the expansion of production a potential solution to upcoming political challenges— whether this was full employment or the hoped-for end to material hardship. Long-term growth of gross national product was *the* political call of the postwar era.

Simultaneously, in the context of the Marshall Plan and emerging development policy, the United States exported to the countries that came under its political influence not only the idea of gross national product and its method of calculation but also, with it, its own ideology of growth. In this way, a largely uniform method of quantifying and interpreting the state of the economy predominated on a global scale. Gross national product, expressed either as a per capita figure or a growth rate, became the standard reference to describe the state of a country, in condensed form.

Indeed, the level of gross national product or per capita income was an indicator of political, economic, and also military power. Growth statistics enabled the number-based comparison of American society with the Soviet system, but they also showed two more things: first, that the United States was the international standard of economic power on which all other states (at least in the Western world) were to orient themselves; and second, that it was possible for every country on earth to achieve the same material well-being as America—provided that these countries sustained the growth of gross national product. The long-term goal was an international alignment of living conditions. That also went for developing countries.

The belief in the importance of perpetual growth was self-reinforcing. In the first decades after World War II, not only did many countries achieve full employment and an increase in material living standards, on the back of the expansion of production, but also a hitherto inconceivable social transformation occurred, as portrayed by Galbraith and Erhard. Growth had led to the modernization of society, had put an end to the decades-long ideological conflicts over distribution, revolution, and solving the "social question"—the widespread poverty that had shaped industrialized nations. Growth saw the arrival of that which, centuries earlier, Petty had suggested be taken as the motto for successful government work: a life in "peace and plenty." It also seemed that classical economists such as Adam Smith, Alfred Marshall, and Arthur Pigou had been right in opining that the expansion of production was a key to solving social problems.

It can thus be said that gross national product and its desired growth never served as a purely informational tool. Its acceptance in the political arena was dependent on certain political objectives. That these objectives actually could be achieved by expanding production, as indeed it seemed at first, further cemented the position of gross national product. Only its growth, according to the political dogma that soon followed, could guarantee resolution of the myriad problems facing society, and a state that was able to cite a high national product or per capita income would earn international respect.

Even putting aside the political goals associated with gross national product and GDP, there are still clear reasons why GDP continues to be accepted in the world of politics. In itself, it provides a seemingly objective overview of economic processes that is purportedly free of ideology and value judgments; it is based on numbers alone. It is determined and measured in line with transparent and understandable criteria. The fact that GDP combines a great many individual aggregates in a single figure signifies an unparalleled information density in public statistics. And because GDP can be determined quickly, for annual periods and even quarters, it is more useful for governments than data that can be determined only in the long term.

Gross national product, according to a view first stated in a 1949 introduction to the measure that is still widespread today, "has proved to be very useful in understanding and explaining what takes place in the economy."[7] Joseph Schumpeter was not so certain about this, however. For him, national product was "a figment which, unlike the price level, would not as such exist at all, were there no statisticians to create it. We seem indeed to be faced by a meaningless heap. . . . for most purposes, a highly inconvenient composite."[8]

As described at the outset, Sarkozy likewise criticized the cult of numbers evoked by the belief in the necessity of growth. People had confused GDP figures with reality, he bemoaned. Lionel Robbins had written something similar back in the 1930s, when he pointed out that the calculation of national income was simply a convention.

This convention is the result of a long political conditioning process, within which it has become common practice to understand gross national product statistics as a realistic depiction of economic processes. The more gross national product became part of the political culture of the Western world, the more people forgot the background of its origins and calculation. Moshe Syrquin describes what then happened as follows: "Once [national accounts are] available, it is easy, and tempting, to forget that they are artificial constructs aggregating the results of myriads of decisions by individual agents into an aggregate devoid of volition or agency."[9]

Simon Kuznets's objections—namely, that an international calculating convention levels the world's diversity and, indeed, that it is impossible to compare different countries by means of an aggregate number—hindered attempts to establish gross national product calculation as the international standard. A further hindrance, from the government's point of view, was voiced by Kuznets and Clark, who questioned whether state activities should influence the calculation of gross national product. Yet the most troublesome factor obstructing the establishment of the political arithmetic of GDP was Kuznets's call for a continual revision of the sense and purpose of all economic activity and, because ideas about what economic activities *are* rest on a consensus that is subject to change, for measuring methods to be adjusted correspondingly.

For Kuznets, human beings and their welfare were at the center of economic activity. For that reason, he wanted the calculation of national income to be geared to the level of income people were receiving. To restrict the calculation to a value of the quantity of goods produced disregards this aspect entirely.[10] The important thing for Kuznets was whether a country's welfare changes over the course of time—not the number of goods produced for the market.[11]

The current international efforts to establish a separate statistical measurement of a society's welfare, parallel to or even in place of GDP, shows how right Kuznets's ideas were and how necessary are such discussions—discussions which Gilbert and, long before him, Petty dismissed as philosophical or moral. Indeed, the essence of these attempts to find a different measure of human well-being is an elementary questioning of the meaning of all economic activity. GDP is, after all, just one way of describing the "perplexed and intricate ways of the World," and it is seemingly no longer a description that satisfies everybody.

GDP and the idea of growth originated in a particular era, marked by particular geopolitical circumstances and challenges. It was the interplay of these circumstances that led to the political establishment of these concepts. Knowledge of the origins of GDP should prompt reflection among all those who reflexively believe that growth in GDP is a suitable approach to overcoming the challenges of the twenty-first century. At the same time, however, the success story of GDP shows those who hope for the rise of an alternative model to GDP just how difficult it will be to repeat its triumph and to break the power of the single number.

NOTES

INTRODUCTION

1. Bureau of Economic Analysis (U.S. Department of Commerce), "GDP: One of the Greatest Inventions of the 20th Century," *Survey of Current Business* 80, no. 1 (2000): 6–14.
2. Joseph Stiglitz, Amartya Sen, and Jean-Paul Fitoussi, *Mismeasuring Our Lives: Why GDP Doesn't Add Up* (London: New Press, 2010), ix.
3. Nikolas Rose and Peter Miller, "Political Power Beyond the State: Problematics of Government," *British Journal of Sociology* 43, no. 2 (1992): 172–205.
4. See, above all, Paul Studenski, *The Income of Nations: Theory, Measurement, and Analysis, Past and Present* (New York: New York University Press, 1958); and André Vanoli, *A History of National Accounting* (Amsterdam: IOS Press, 2005).

1. WHAT IT'S ALL ABOUT: A SHORT PRIMER ON GDP

1. Federal Statistical Office of Germany (Destatis), *Statistical Yearbook* (Wiesbaden: Statistisches Bundesamt, 2012), 339, https://www.destatis.de/DE/Publikationen/StatistischesJahrbuch/Statistisches Jahrbuch2012.pdf.
2. See the explanation on the website of the Federal Statistical Office of Germany (Destatis): https://www.destatis.de/DE/ZahlenFakten /GesamtwirtschaftUmwelt/VGR/Methoden/BIP.html.
3. Initially, only the basic price is recorded—the price that a producer receives from the end consumer, without value-added tax. Gross value

added is then calculated as an accumulation of these basic prices. Adding taxes on goods (these might include a value-added tax or, for example, a gasoline tax) and subtracting possible subsidies for goods results in value added at market prices and, by definition, gross domestic product.

4. In theory, GDP can increase not only through the volume of produced goods and services but also through improvements in the quality of goods, which is reflected in a higher price. The method of recording the difference between improved quality and straightforward inflation is, however, very difficult in terms of methodology. See, in this context, *Abschlussbericht der Projektgruppe 1: Stellenwert von Wachstum in Wirtschaft und Gesellschaft—Oppositionsbericht*, in German Parliamentary Enquete Commission, "Growth, Prosperity and Quality of Life" (printed committee report 17 [26] 84, Berlin, 2013), http://dip21 .bundestag.de/dip21/btd/17/133/1713300.pdf. Of greater consequence here is the fact that, historically, the valuation of the quantity of goods produced and services rendered was, and indeed still is, associated with the idea of growth.

5. In Germany, the term "gross national product" is now rarely used; it has been replaced by the term "gross national income."

6. See the Federal Statistical Office of Germany (Destatis), https:// www.destatis.de/DE/ZahlenFakten/GesamtwirtschaftUmwelt/VGR /Methoden/BIP.html.

7. Destatis, *Statistical Yearbook*, 337.

2. WILLIAM PETTY AND POLITICAL ARITHMETIC: THE ORIGINS OF GDP

1. C. H. Hull, *The Economic Writings of William Petty*, vol. 1 (Cambridge: Cambridge University Press, 1899), xxxiii.

2. Bertram Schefold et al., *Vademecum zu einem Klassiker der angewandten Nationalökonomie* (Düsseldorf: Wirtschaft und Finanzen, 1992), 97.

3. Antoin E. Murphy, *The Genesis of Macroeconomics: New Ideas from Sir William Petty to Henry Thornton* (Oxford: Oxford University Press, 2009), 23.

4. Murphy, *Genesis of Macroeconomics*, 21–22.

5. Stephen Gaukroner, *Francis Bacon and the Transformation of Early-Modern Philosophy* (Cambridge: Cambridge University Press, 2001).

6. Hull, *Economic Writings*, 1:xl.

7. C. H. Hull, *The Economic Writings of William Petty*, vol. 2 (Cambridge: Cambridge University Press, 1899), 394.

8. Hull, *Economic Writings*, 2:395–397. Following a plague epidemic in the mid-seventeenth century, a Parliamentary resolution declared that all communities in England and Wales were obliged to keep detailed registers of births and deaths. In addition, changes to the tax system ensured that, for the first time, data relating to property, land ownership, farm animals, and food consumption was collected. Foreign trade was also subjected to more rigorous controls and the flows of goods was registered, such that during Petty's lifetime there was a data pool covering economic and social circumstances, albeit an incomplete and rudimentary one. Never before had better information been available.

9. William Petty, *The Political Anatomy of Ireland* (London, 1691).

10. Hull, *Economic Writings*, 1:lxxiii.

11. John W. Kendrick, "The Historical Development of National-Income Accounts," *History of Political Economy* 2, no. 2 (1970): 286.

12. In his 1662 *Treatise of Taxes and Contributions*, Petty had estimated expenditure by the British people to be "probably not less than 50 million." See Hull, *Economic Writings*, 1:56.

13. Murphy, *Genesis of Macroeconomics*, 31.

14. See Karl Marx, *Das Kapital*, in *Marx-Engels-Werke (MEW)*, vol. 23 (Berlin: Dietz, 1962), 908; and Friedrich Engels, *Herrn Eugen Dührings Umwälzung der Wissenschaft* [1878], in *Marx-Engels Werke*, vol. 20, 216 and 218.

15. Hull, *Economic Writings*, 1:lxv. See also Theodore M. Porter, *The Rise of Statistical Thinking, 1820–1900* (Princeton: Princeton University Press, 1986), 19.

16. Hull, *Economic Writings*, 1:xxx.

17. Ibid., 302–303.

18. Ibid., 240.

19. Ibid., 239–240. See also Paul Studenski, *The Income of Nations: Theory, Measurement, and Analysis, Past and Present* (New York: New York University Press, 1958), 29.

20. Schefold et al., *Vademecum*, 63.

21. Murphy, *Genesis of Macroeconomics*, 28.

22. Peter Miller, "Governing by Numbers: Why Calculative Practices Matter," *Social Research* 68, no. 2 (2001): 379–396.

23. For a detailed account of the historical calculations, see Studenski, *Income of Nations*. Compared to Petty's writings, however, most of these estimations had little political influence.

24. Adam Smith, *The Wealth of Nations*, vol. 2 (London: Penguin Classics, 1999 [1776]), 114.

25. Adam Smith, *The Wealth of Nations*, vol. 1 (London: Penguin Classics, 1982 [1776]), 115.
26. Ibid., 441.
27. Ibid., 117.
28. Ibid., 443.
29. André Vanoli, *A History of National Accounting* (Amsterdam: IOS Press, 2005), 12.
30. Smith, *Wealth of Nations*, 2:32.
31. Ibid.
32. Adam Smith, *The Theory of Moral Sentiments* (Indianapolis: Liberty Fund, 1976 [1759]).
33. Salim Rashid, "Malthus' Principles and British Economic Thought, 1820–1835," *History of Political Economy* 13, no. 1 (1981): 55–79.
34. Alfred Marshall, *Principles of Economics*, 8th ed. (New York: Cosimo Classics, 2009 [1890]). According to Marshall's definition, "Political Economy or Economics is a study of mankind in the ordinary business of life; it examines that part of individual and social action which is most closely connected with the attainment and with the use of the material requisites of wellbeing" (1). Economics was the examination of wealth, but primarily the analysis of human behavior.
35. Marshall, *Principles of Economics*, 434. Marshall used the term "national income" as well as "national dividend."
36. Ibid., 47.
37. Pigou uses the term "national dividend" rather than "national income."
38. Arthur Cecil Pigou, *The Economics of Welfare* (London: Macmillan, 1932 [1920]), 11.
39. Ibid., 12.
40. Ibid., 31.
41. Ibid., 33.
42. Lionel Robbins, *An Essay on the Nature and Significance of Economic Science* (London: Macmillan, 1945 [1932]), 46.

3. THE FRUSTRATIONS OF
COLIN CLARK: ENGLAND

1. Gerald M. Meier and Dudley Seers, eds., *Pioneers in Development* (New York: Oxford University Press, 1984).
2. Angus Maddison, "Macromeasurement Before and After Colin Clark" (Colin Clark Lecture, University of Queensland, August 22, 2003), 2, http://www.ggdc.net/Maddison/articles/colin_clark.pdf.

3. Ibid., 9.
4. George Peters, *Colin Clark (1905–89): Economist and Agricultural Economist* (working paper no. 69, QEH Working Paper Series, University of Oxford, 2001), 2.
5. Colin Clark, *The National Income, 1924–1931* (London: Macmillan, 1932).
6. Colin Clark, *National Income and Outlay* (London: Macmillan, 1937).
7. Colin Clark, *The Conditions of Economic Progress* (London: Macmillan, 1940).
8. John W. Kendrick, "The Historical Development of National-Income Accounts," *History of Political Economy* 2, no. 2 (1970): 304.
9. See Paul Studenski, *The Income of Nations: Theory, Measurement, and Analysis, Past and Present* (New York: New York University Press, 1958), 136; and André Vanoli, *A History of National Accounting* (Amsterdam: IOS Press, 2005), 15.
10. In the last part of his life, Clark gained scholarly recognition not for his calculations of national income but for his writings on agricultural economics. For a long time they were considered standard works. See, for example, Colin Clark and Margaret Haswell, *The Economics of Subsistence Agriculture* (London: Macmillan, 1964).
11. Maddison, "Macromeasurement," 12.
12. Colin Clark, *Population Growth and Land Use* (London: Macmillan, 1967).
13. Colin Clark, "Development Economics: The Early Years," in Meier and Seers, eds., *Pioneers in Development*, 59.
14. Clark, *The National Income*, 118.
15. Ibid., vi.
16. Ibid., 83.
17. Alec Cairncross, "The Development of Economic Statistics as an Influence on Theory and Policy," in *National Income and Economic Progress: Essays in Honour of Colin Clark*, ed. Duncan Ironmonger, J. O. N. Perkins, and Tran Van Hoa (London: Macmillan, 1988), 11.
18. Clark, *National Income and Outlay*, vii.
19. In his analyses, Clark ascertained that the rural areas of the Soviet Union were relatively underpopulated. According to Clark, a population increase of 25 percent in just ten years was the reason for most of Russia's economic problems. The "ghost of Malthus" seemed to haunt Russia. Clark was unable to abstain from a moral judgment: "Russia with its comparatively large stretches of infertile soil and its still fertile marriage-beds, as one of the countries where the Devil still holds sway, unexorcised

by Marxian dialectic" (Colin Clark, *A Critique of Russian Statistics* [London: MacMillan, 1939], 51). However, developments in the last years of his study, the early 1930s, gave Clark hope. Russia's industrial production had risen, absorbing the workforce from the agricultural sector, while according to his calculations per capita income rose. "The Malthusian devil is being cornered" (69), as Clark put it.

20. Clark, *Critique*, 2.
21. Clark, *Conditions*, vii.
22. Maddison, "Macromeasurement," 14–15.
23. Clark, *Conditions*, cover.
24. Ibid., viii.
25. Ibid., x.
26. Ibid., viii. See also Maddison, "Macromeasurement," 16.
27. Clark, *Conditions*, 2.
28. Ibid., 1.
29. According to John Kendrick, a similar comparison was made in 1884, in England, in M. G. Mulhall's *Dictionary of Statistics*, though it was limited to eighteen countries. An attempt also had been made to base the comparison on a uniform currency and to produce per capita figures. See Kendrick, "Historical Development," 302.
30. Clark, *Conditions*, 39–41. Nowadays, international comparisons of different per capita incomes or gross domestic products are based mostly on purchasing power parity, determined on the basis of price comparisons, for which an international basket of goods is used. These exchange rates enable statements to be made about different economic capacity in a direct comparison of countries.
31. Ibid., 2–4, 53.
32. Ibid., 29.
33. H. W. Arndt, "Colin Clark," in Ironmonger, Perkins, and Tran, eds., *National Income*, 2.
34. Ibid., 4.
35. Maddison, "Macromeasurement," 27.
36. Cairncross, "Development of Economic Statistics," 12.
37. Don Patinkin, "Keynes and Econometrics: On the Interaction Between the Macroeconomic Revolutions of the Interwar Period," *Econometrica* 44, no. 6 (1976): 1109.
38. John Maynard Keynes, *The General Theory of Employment, Interest, and Money* (London: Macmillan, 1973 [1936]), 40.
39. Lionel Robbins, *An Essay on the Nature and Significance of Economic Science* (London: Macmillan and Co., 1945 [1932]), ix–x.

40. Vanoli, *History of National Accounting*, 20; and Patinkin, "Keynes and Econometrics," 1110.
41. John Maynard Keynes, *How to Pay for the War* (London: Macmillan, 1940), 13.
42. Ibid., 79.
43. Keynes, *General Theory*, 63.
44. Benjamin Mitra-Kahn, *Redefining the Economy: A History of Economics and National Accounting* (unpublished dissertation, City University London, 2009), 211, http://mitrakahn.files.wordpress.com/2011/11 /mitra-kahn-autumn-2011-final.pdf.
45. Erwin Rothbarth, "Income and Fiscal Potentials of Great Britain," *Economic Journal* 49, no. 196 (1939): 627.
46. Keynes, *How to Pay*, 13. See also Patinkin, "Keynes and Econometrics," 1115.
47. Keynes, *How to Pay*, 13.
48. Mitra-Kahn, *Redefining the Economy*, 216.
49. Ron Harrod, *The Life of John Maynard Keynes* (New York: Norton, 1982 [1951]), 503.
50. Angus Deaton, "John Richard Nicholas Stone 1913–1991," *Proceedings of the British Academy* 65 (2002): 475–492.
51. James Meade and Richard Stone, "The Construction of Tables of National Income, Expenditure, Savings, and Investment," *Economic Journal* 51, no. 202–203 (1941): 216.
52. Ibid., 218.
53. Moshe Syrquin, *GDP as a Measure of Economic Welfare* (working paper no. 3, International Center for Economic Research, Turin, 2011).
54. Meade and Stone, "Construction," 216.
55. Y. Kurabayashi, "Keynes' *How to Pay for the War* and its Influence on Post-War National Accounting," in *The Accounts of Nations*, ed. Zoltan Kenessey (Amsterdam: IOS Press, 1994), 93–108.
56. Mitra-Kahn, *Redefining the Economy*, 224.
57. Cairncross, "Development of Economic Statistics," 15.
58. Vanoli, *History of National Accounting*, 19.

4. SIMON KUZNETS AND THE POLITICS OF GROSS NATIONAL PRODUCT: THE UNITED STATES

1. Simon Kuznets, "Economic Growth and Income Inequality," *American Economic Review* 45, no. 1 (1955): 1–28.
2. H. W. Arndt, "The Trickle-Down Myth," *Economic Development and Cultural Change* 32, no. 1 (1983): 1–10.

3. Vibha Kapuria-Foreman and Mark Perlman, "An Economic Historian's Economist: Remembering Simon Kuznets," *Economic Journal* 105, no. 433 (1995): 1524.

4. Malcolm Rutherford, "Who's Afraid of Arthur Burns? The NBER and the Foundations," *Journal of the History of Economic Thought* 27, no. 2 (2005): 111.

5. Nikolai Kondratieff, "Die langen Wellen der Konjunktur," *Archiv für Sozialwissenschaft und Sozialpolitik* 56, no. 3 (1926): 573–609.

6. Alongside Kuznets, this generation included, for example, economists such as Alexander Gerschenkron, Albert O. Hirschman, and Joseph Schumpeter.

7. Angus Maddison, "Contours of the World Economy and the Art of Macro-measurement 1500–2001" (Ruggles Lecture, IARIW 28th General Conference, Cork, August 2004), 10, http://www.ggdc.net/Maddison /articles/ruggles.pdf.

8. Kuznets, "Economic Growth and Income Inequality," 28.

9. Kapuria-Foreman and Perlman, "An Economic Historian's Economist," 1525, 1545.

10. Rosemary D. Marcuss and Richard E. Kane, "U.S. National Income and Product Statistics: Born of the Great Depression and World War II," *Survey of Current Business* 87, no. 2 (2007): 32.

11. Carol Carson, "The History of the United States National Income and Product Accounts: The Development of an Analytical Tool," *Review of Income and Wealth* 21 (1975): 156.

12. United States Senate, *Establishment of National Economic Council: Hearings Before a Subcommittee of the Committee on Manufactures, United States Senate, Seventy-second Congress, First Session, on S. 6215 (71st Congress)* (Washington, DC: U.S. Government Printing Office, 1932), 566–587.

13. Ibid., 583.

14. Carson, "History," 156; and United States Senate, "Estimates of National Income and its Distribution," *Journal of the Senate* 27 (Congress, first session, 1932): 556–567.

15. Rutherford, "Who's Afraid of Arthur Burns?," 117.

16. Kapuria-Foreman and Perlman, "An Economic Historian's Economist," 1529.

17. Simon Kuznets, "National Income," in *Encyclopaedia of the Social Sciences*, vol. 11, ed. Edwin Seligman and Alvin Johnson (New York: Macmillan, 1933): 205.

18. Ibid., 207.

19. Ibid., 205–206.
20. Ibid., 224.
21. Ibid., 205.
22. Kapuria-Foreman and Perlman, "An Economic Historian's Economist," 1530.
23. Kuznets, "National Income," 209.
24. In this, Kuznets was probably heavily influenced by the work of the Russian agricultural statistician Alexander Chayanov, who as long ago as the early twentieth century had described the way Russian farming families lived and worked as family economies, and who wanted to record their economic rationality.
25. Simon Kuznets, *National Income, 1929–1932* (New York: National Bureau of Economic Research, 1934).
26. Marcuss and Kane, "U.S. National Income," 34.
27. Ibid.
28. Ibid., 35.
29. Simon Kuznets, *National Income and Capital Formation, 1919–1935* (New York: National Bureau of Economic Research, 1937), 3, 6.
30. Carson, "History," 160.
31. Marcuss and Kane, "U.S. National Income," 36.
32. Clark Warburton, "Value of the Gross National Product and Its Components, 1919–1929," *Journal of the American Statistical Association* 29, no. 188 (1934): 383–388. In 1937, Kuznets had used the term "gross national product" in *National Income and Capital Formation, 1919–1935*, but had not accorded it any major significance.
33. Carson, "History," 166. See also Byrd L. Jones, "The Role of Keynesians in Wartime Policy and Postwar Planning, 1940–1946," *American Economic Review* 62, no. 2 (1972): 125–133.
34. Benjamin Mitra-Kahn, *Redefining the Economy: A History of Economics and National Accounting* (unpublished dissertation, City University London, 2009), 254, http://mitrakahn.files.wordpress.com/2011/11/mitra-kahn-autumn-2011-final.pdf.
35. Mitra-Kahn, *Redefining the Economy*, 260.
36. See Milton Gilbert and George Jaszi, "National Product and Income Statistics as an Aid in Economic Problems," *Dun's Review* (February 1944): 9–12 and 30–38; and Marcuss and Kane, "U.S. National Income," 37.
37. Carson, "History," 169.
38. Milton Gilbert, "War Expenditures and National Production," *Survey of Current Business* 22, no. 3 (1942): 9.
39. Gilbert, "War Expenditures," 10.

40. Marcuss and Kane, "U.S. National Income," 38.
41. Carson, "History," 170. See also Simon Kuznets, "National Income: A New Version," *Review of Economics and Statistics* 30, no. 3 (1948): 151–179; and Milton Gilbert et al., "Objective of National Income Measurement: A Reply to Professor Kuznets, *Review of Economics and Statistics* 30, no. 3 (1948): 179–195.
42. Gilbert, "War Expenditures," 12.
43. Marcuss and Kane, "U.S. National Income," 40.
44. André Vanoli, *A History of National Accounting* (Amsterdam: IOS Press, 2005), 22.
45. Gilbert and Jaszi, "National Product."
46. Ibid., 37.
47. Marcuss and Kane, "U.S. National Income," 41.
48. Simon Kuznets, *National Product in Wartime* (New York: National Bureau of Economic Research, 1945), vii.
49. Ibid., x.
50. Ibid., 21.
51. Ibid., 26–27.
52. Ibid., 27.
53. Ibid., 31.
54. Milton Gilbert et al., "National Product, War and Prewar: Some Comments on Professor Kuznets' Study and a Reply by Professor Kuznets," *Review of Economic Statistics* 26, no. 3 (1944): 109, 118.
55. Ibid., 135.
56. Edward F. Denison, "Report on Tripartite Discussions of National Income Measurement," *Studies in Income and Wealth* 10 (1947): 21. The peculiarities of the American and English accounts systems, which did not totally correspond, are not described in detail here.
57. Ibid., 4.
58. Vanoli, *History of National Accounting*, 26.
59. Simon Kuznets, "Measurement of Economic Growth," *Journal of Economic History* 7 (1947): 18.
60. Kuznets, "National Income: A New Version."
61. Ibid., 156–163.
62. Ibid., 153.
63. Gilbert et al., "Objective of National Income Measurement," 179. Since 1936, academic discussions on the methodology of national income and gross domestic product have been held at the Conference on Research in Income and Wealth, which was created by the National Bureau of Eco-

nomic Research. Since 1949, discussions have also taken place within the Association of Research in Income and Wealth.

64. Ibid., 189.

5. WAR, KIDNAPPING, AND DATA THEFT: GERMANY

1. Colin Clark, *The Conditions of Economic Progress* (London: Macmillan, 1940), 374.

2. Paul Studenski, *The Income of Nations: Theory, Measurement, and Analysis, Past and Present* (New York: New York University Press, 1958), 135.

3. Ibid., 144.

4. Ibid., 60.

5. Adam Tooze, *Statistics and the German State, 1900–1945: The Making of Modern Economic Knowledge* (Cambridge: Cambridge University Press, 2001), 40ff. Most of the information used here on the history of German statistics until the Nazi era is based on this work.

6. Ibid., 64.

7. Ibid., 70. It was not until around the end of the war that the Imperial Economics Office and the Imperial Employment Office became established as central authorities of the economic administration of the empire. The Statistical Office was merged with the Economics Office.

8. Ibid., 79.

9. Ibid., 84.

10. Ibid., 90.

11. Ibid., 95.

12. Adam Tooze, "Weimar's Statistical Economics: Ernst Wagemann, the Reich's Statistical Office, and the Institute for Business-Cycle Research, 1925–1933, *Economic History Review* 52, no. 3 (1999): 527.

13. Rolf Krengel, *Das Deutsche Institut für Wirtschaftsforschung (Institut für Konjunkturforschung) 1925–1979* (Berlin: Duncker and Humblot, 1986), 12ff.

14. Karl Diehl et al., "Diskussionsprotokoll bei der Sitzung des Ständigen Unterausschusses," in *Beiträge zur Wirtschaftstheorie. Teil 1: Volkseinkommen und Volksvermögen* (Verein für Socialpolitik essays 173, no. 1), ed. Karl Diehl (Munich: Duncker und Humblot, 1926), 156. For a detailed analysis of this dispute, see Daniel Speich Chassé, *Welt des Bruttosozialprodukts: Globale Ungleichheit in der Wissensgeschichte der Ökonomie* (unpublished thesis, Zurich, 2012). The Diehl quotation is on page 60.

15. Joseph Schumpeter, *Business Cycles: A Theoretical, Historical, and Statistical Analysis of the Capitalist Process*, vol. 2 (New York: McGraw-Hill, 1939), 561.

16. Stefan Hauf and Klaus Voy, "Produktions- und Einkommensbegriffe der Volkswirtschaftlichen Gesamtrechnungen," in *Kategorien der Volkswirtschaftlichen Gesamtrechnungen. Band 4: Zur Geschichte der Volkswirtschaftlichen Gesamtrechnungen nach 1945*, ed. Klaus Voy (Marburg: Metropolis, 2009), 150.

17. Ernst Wagemann, *Struktur und Rhythmus der Weltwirtschaft: Grundlagen einer weltwirtschaftlichen Konjunkturlehre* (Berlin: Reimar Hobbing, 1931).

18. Krengel, *Das Deutsche Institut*, 25. Compare, however, Tooze, *Statistics and the German State*, 144.

19. Tooze, *Statistics and the German State*, 152ff.

20. Ernest Doblin, "Measuring German National Income in Wartime," *Studies in Income and Wealth*, 8 (1946): 175–194.

21. Tooze, *Statistics and the German State*, 190.

22. Rainer Fremdling and Reiner Stäglin, *Der Industriezensus von 1936 als Grundlage einer neuen Volkswirtschaftlichen Gesamtrechnung für Deutschland* (working paper 41, Thünen Series of Applied Economic Theory, Universität Rostock, 2003), 9.

23. Fremdling and Stäglin, *Der Industriezensus von 1936*, 10.

24. Tooze, *Statistics and the German State*, 248.

25. British Intelligence Objective Subcommittee (BIOS), *Symposium of Interrogations and Reports on German Methods of Statistical Reporting* (final report no. 273, London, 1946), 74.

26. Krengel, *Das Deutsche Institut*, 64, 67. See also Deutsches Institut für Wirtschaftsforschung (DIW), *Gelehrtenrepublik und Denkfabrik: Das Deutsche Institut für Wirtschaftsforschung 1925–2012* (Berlin: DIW, 2012), 21.

27. Krengel, *Das Deutsche Institut*, 45.

28. Hans Kehrl, *Krisenmanager im Dritten Reich: 6 Jahre Frieden, 6 Jahre Krieg—Erinnerungen* (Düsseldorf: Droste, 1973), 12. See also Krengel, *Das Deutsche Institut*, 68.

29. Tooze, *Statistics and the German State*, 268.

30. Ibid., 273.

31. John Kenneth Galbraith, "The National Accounts: Arrival and Impact," in *Reflections of America: Commemorating the Statistical Abstract Centennial*, ed. Norman Cousins (Washington, DC: U.S. Department of Commerce, Bureau of the Census, 1980), 77.

32. John Kenneth Galbraith, *A Life in Our Times: Memoirs* (Boston: Houghton Mifflin, 1981), 199.

33. Angus Maddison, "Contours of the World Economy and the Art of Macro-measurement 1500–2001" (Ruggles Lecture, IARIW 28th General Conference, Cork, August 2004), 32, http://www.ggdc.net /Maddison/articles/ruggles.pdf.

34. Hildegard Bartels, Utz-Peter Reich, and Heinrich Lützel, "Aus den Anfängen der Westdeutschen Volkswirtschaftlichen Gesamtrechnungen nach dem Krieg," in Voy, ed., *Kategorien der Volkswirtschaftlichen Gesamtrechnungen*, 512.

35. Galbraith, *A Life in Our Times*, 222.

36. Ibid.

37. Jürgen Kuczynski, "Rolf Wagenführ: Ein edler Ritter der Statistik," in *Probleme internationaler wirtschafts- und sozialstatistischer Vergleiche: Rolf Wagenführ zum Gedächtnis*, ed. Günter Menges and Reiner Zwer (Cologne: Bund-Verlag, 1981), 11–14. In his memoirs, Kuczynski describes his work on the survey, and speaks openly of his dislike of Galbraith, but does not disclose the reasons for his journey to Berlin. He considered it worth imparting, however, that he used his visit to Berlin to make contact with Walter Ulbricht. See Jürgen Kuczynski, *Memoiren: Die Erziehung des J. K. zum Kommunisten und Wissenschaftler* (Berlin: Aufbau-Verlag and Weimar, 1972).

38. Wagenführ himself used the data to later publish his book *Die Deutsche Industrie im Kriege 1939–1945* (Berlin: Duncker and Humblot, 1954). See also the article by his old "superior" at the Ministry of Armaments, Hans Kehrl, "Rolf Wagenführ im Institut für Konjunkturforschung," in Menges and Zwer, *Probleme internationaler*, 9.

39. Galbraith, *A Life in Our Times*, 201.

40. Galbraith, "The National Accounts," 80.

41. Alexander Nützenadel, *Stunde der Ökonomen: Wissenschaft, Politik und Expertenkultur in der Bundesrepublik 1949–1974* (Göttingen: Vandenhoeck und Ruprecht, 2005), 99.

42. Until 1950, the French zone had its own statistical organization. It was not possible to establish the Federal Statistical Office until this organization was closed.

43. Carsten Stahmer, "Organisatorischer Neuanfang und erste Berechnungen: Frühgeschichte der Volkswirtschaftlichen Gesamtrechnungen in Westdeutschland," in Voy, ed., *Kategorien der Volkswirtschaftlichen Gesamtrechnungen*, 78–79.

44. Gerhard Fürst and Hildegard Bartels, "Social Accounts and Calculation of National Income in Germany (Bizonal Area)," in Voy, ed., *Kategorien der Volkswirtschaftlichen Gesamtrechnungen*, 528.

45. Stahmer, "Organisatorischer Neuanfang," 74.

46. Bartels, Reich, and Lützel, "Aus den Anfängen," 512.

47. Otto Schörry, "Volkseinkommen, Sozialprodukt und Zahlungsbilanz des Bundesgebietes im ersten Marshallplanjahr 1948/49," *Wirtschaft und Statistik* 1, no. 9 (1949): 256–261.

48. Otto Schörry, "Volkseinkommen und Sozialprodukt des Vereinigten Wirtschaftsgebiets im Jahre 1936 und im zweiten Halbjahr 1948," *Wirtschaft und Statistik* 1, no. 3 (1949): 94.

49. Hildegard Bartels, "Reallohn- und Sozialprodukt," *Wirtschaft und Statistik* 1, no. 4 (1949): 66.

50. Cited in Nützenadel, *Stunde der Ökonomen*, 102.

51. Bartels, Reich, and Lützel, "Aus den Anfängen," 509.

52. François Fourquet, *Les comptes de la puissance* (Paris: Editions Recherches, 1980).

53. Bartels, Reich, and Lützel, "Aus den Anfängen," 508.

6. THE ULTIMATE TRIUMPH OF GROSS NATIONAL PRODUCT

1. Russell F. Weigley, *The American Way of War: A History of United States Military Strategy and Policy* (Bloomington: Indiana University Press, 1973), 146.

2. John Kenneth Galbraith, "The National Accounts: Arrival and Impact," in *Reflections of America: Commemorating the Statistical Abstract Centennial*, ed. Norman Cousins (Washington, DC: U.S. Department of Commerce, Bureau of the Census, 1980), 76.

3. A scenario that Harvard economist Alvin Hansen had prominently put forward in 1938.

4. Colin Clark, *Growthmanship* (Barnet, UK: Institute for Economic Affairs, 1961).

5. Simon Kuznets, *Toward a Theory of Economic Growth* (New York: Norton, 1968 [1953]), 2.

6. Robert Collins, *More: The Politics of Economic Growth in Postwar America* (Oxford: Oxford University Press, 2000), 18.

7. Ibid., 22. The term "politics of productivity" comes from Charles S. Meier.

8. Ibid., 32.

9. Ibid., 35.

10. John Kenneth Galbraith, *A Life in Our Times: Memoirs* (Boston: Houghton Mifflin, 1981), 248.

11. Hildegard Bartels, Utz-Peter Reich, and Heinrich Lützel, "Aus den Anfängen der Westdeutschen Volkswirtschaftlichen Gesamtrechnungen nach dem Krieg," in *Kategorien der Volkswirtschaftlichen Gesamtrechnungen. Band 4: Zur Geschichte der Volkswirtschaftlichen Gesamtrechnungen nach 1945*, ed. Klaus Voy (Marburg: Metropolis, 2009), 507.

12. Richard Ruggles, "United Nations System of National Accounts (SNA) and the Integration of Macro- and Microdata," in Nancy Ruggles and Richard Ruggles, *National Accounting and Economic Policy: The United States and UN Systems* (London: Edward Elgar, 1999), 497.

13. Angus Maddison, "Contours of the World Economy and the Art of Macro-measurement 1500–2001" (Ruggles Lecture, IARIW 28th General Conference, Cork, August 2004), 1, http://www.ggdc.net/Maddison /articles/ruggles.pdf.

14. As early as 1939, the League of Nations had started collecting data on various countries' national income. World War II interrupted this work. Shortly after the British, Americans, and Canadians agreed on the national income calculation method, the statisticians of the League of Nations, which officially still existed, convened in Princeton, New Jersey, in December 1945, to continue the work started before the war. Here again Richard Stone had a platform where he was able to present his accounts logic to an international audience, which those present accepted as recommendations. In 1947, a report was published by the League of Nations' statistical committee, entitled *Measurement of National-Income and the Construction of Social Accounts*, outlining the method that was later adopted by the United Nations. This report is considered the fundamental work for the international harmonization of national accounts.

15. David Ellwood, "The Marshall Plan and the Politics of Growth," in *Explorations in OEEC History*, ed. Richard Griffiths (Paris: Organisation for Economic Co-operation and Development, 1997), 104.

16. Paul Rosenstein-Rodan, "Problems of Industrialization of Eastern and South-Eastern Europe," *Economic Journal* 53, no. 210/211 (1943), 202–211.

17. Paul Rosenstein-Rodan, "The International Development of Economically Backward Areas," *International Affairs* 20, no. 2 (1944): 159.

18. Ron F. Harrod, "An Essay in Dynamic Theory," *Economic Journal* 49, no. 193 (1939): 256; and H. W. Arndt, *The Rise and Fall of Economic Growth* (Melbourne: Longman Cheshire, 1978), 35.

19. Evsey Domar, "Capital Expansion, Rate of Growth, and Employment," *Econometrica* 14, no. 2 (1946): 147.

20. Arndt, *Rise and Fall*, 33.

21. Arthur Lewis, *The Theory of Economic Growth* (London: Allen and Unwin, 1955), 10.
22. Arndt, *Rise and Fall*, 37.
23. Ellwood, "The Marshall Plan," 105.
24. Harold G. Moulton, *Controlling Factors in Economic Development* (Washington, DC: Brookings Institute, 1949), 143.
25. Kuznets, *Toward a Theory*, 3.
26. Cited in Arndt, *Rise and Fall*, 48.
27. Arndt, *Rise and Fall*, 51.
28. Ibid., 65.
29. Walt Whitman Rostow, *The Stages of Economic Growth: A Non-Communist Manifesto* (Cambridge: Cambridge University Press, 1960).
30. John Kenneth Galbraith, *The Affluent Society* (Harmondsworth, UK: Penguin, 1965 [1958]).
31. Ibid., 76.
32. Ibid., 86.
33. Ibid., 87.
34. Ludwig Erhard, *Prosperity Through Competition*, trans. Edith Temple Roberts and John B. Wood (New York: Praeger, 1958), 1.
35. Ibid., 3–4.
36. Ibid., 4.
37. Ibid., 62.
38. Ibid., 163, 168.
39. Ibid., 169.
40. Ibid., 172.
41. Ibid., 173.

CONCLUSION

1. Particularly noteworthy here is the 1972 Club of Rome report (D. H. Meadows et al., *The Limits of Growth* [New York: Universe Books, 1972]), as well as the "classic" methodological critique of growth in gross national product of the same year: James Tobin and William Nordhaus, "Is Growth Obsolete?," in *Economic Research: Retrospect and Prospect*. Vol. 5: *Economic Growth*, ed. James Tobin and William Nordhaus (New York: National Bureau for Economic Research, 1972), 1–80. For current examples, see also the ideas on *"décroissance"* (degrowth) in Serge Latouche, *Farewell to Growth* (Malden, MA: Polity Press, 2009); or Tim Jackson, *Prosperity Without Growth* (London: Earthscan, 2009), which explores the issue of uncoupling economic growth from

resource consumption. Equally important are the ideas that growth could be "qualitative" in one form or another; see here the approaches of "green economy" or "inclusive green growth," concepts developed by the World Bank and the Organisation for Economic Co-operation and Development.

2. Walt Whitman Rostow, *The Stages of Economic Growth: A Non-Communist Manifesto* (Cambridge: Cambridge University Press, 1960), 70.

3. For an overview of the critical history of GDP/gross national product, see Lorenzo Fioramonti, *Gross Domestic Problem: The Politics Behind the World's Most Powerful Number* (London: Zed Books, 2013).

4. German Parliamentary Enquete Commission, "Growth, Prosperity and Quality of Life" (printed committee report 17 [26] 84, Berlin, 2013), http://dip21.bundestag.de/dip21/btd/17/133/1713300.pdf.

5. David Cameron, "PM Speech on Wellbeing" (delivered November 25, 2010), https://www.gov.uk/government/speeches/pm-speech-on-wellbeing.

6. Rolf Kroker, "Das Bruttoinlandsprodukt hat als Wohlstandsmaß nicht ausgedient!," *Ifo Schnelldienst* 4 (2011): 3–6.

7. Richard Ruggles, *An Introduction to National Income and Income Analysis* (New York: McGraw-Hill, 1949), 3.

8. Joseph Schumpeter, *Business Cycles: A Theoretical, Historical, and Statistical Analysis of the Capitalist Process*, vol. 2 (New York: McGraw-Hill, 1939), 484, 561; cited in Angus Maddison, "Contours of the World Economy and the Art of Macro-measurement 1500–2001" (Ruggles Lecture, IARIW 28th General Conference, Cork, August 2004), 7, http://www.ggdc.net/Maddison/articles/ruggles.pdf.

9. Moshe Syrquin, *GDP as a Measure of Economic Welfare* (working paper no. 3, International Center for Economic Research, Turin, 2011), 6.

10. Simon Kuznets, "National Income and Economic Welfare," in *Economic Change: Selected Essays in Business Cycles, National Income, and Economic Growth* (New York: Norton, 1953), 59–60; cited in Syrquin, *GDP as a Measure of Economic Welfare*, 6.

11. Simon Kuznets, "Measurement of Economic Growth," *Journal of Economic History* 7 (1947): 25.

INDEX

Terborgh, George, 125
Theory of Economic Growth (Lewis),
131–134
Tomorrow Without Fear (Bowles),
125–126
Tooze, Adam, 99–100, 104, 113
"Tragedy of the Commons, The"
(Hardin), 36
Truman, Harry S., 137

unemployment, 124–125. *See also*
employment
United Nations: comparative
study of gross national product
calculations, 137; Development
Programme, 148; System of National Accounts, 5–6, 51, 129
United States: affluence of, 44;
alternative indicators sought,
148; annual growth rate target
(1960s), 138; armaments and
military spending, 76–83, 86,
123; competition with Soviet
Union, 136–137, 152; economists
and economic science in, 61 (*see
also specific individuals*); gross
national product adopted as
measure, 78–86, 123; gross national product concept exported, 113–121, 152; gross national
product's growing political importance, 125–126, 151–152; and
the international harmonization
of accounts systems, 92, 95, 129,
171n14; as international standard
of economic power, 152; national
accounts system, 65–66, 74–78,
90–96, 129 (*see also* Kuznets,
Simon); national income calculation in, 47–50, 57, 60–66,

78–79, 151 (*see also* Gilbert,
Milton; gross national product;
Kuznets, Simon; national
income); postwar transition
to peacetime economy, 85–86,
123–125. *See also* Commerce, U.S.
Dept. of; Congress, U.S.; *and
specific topics and individuals*

value (defined), 1–2, 157–158n3
"Verbum Sapienti" (Petty), 14–16
Verien für Socialpolitik (Ger-
man economists' association),
105–106
Viner, Jacob, 63

Wagemann, Ernst, 103–105, 107, 108.
See also Institute for Business-
Cycle Research; Reich Statistical
Office
Wagenführ, Rolf, 111–112, 115–117,
169n38
Warburton, Clark, 75
wartime economy. *See* peacetime vs.
wartime economy; World War I;
World War II
wealth: and income inequality,
139–140, 143 (*see also* inequality); international disparities, 44,
132–133; Marshall on creation
of, 27–28; Robbins on relevance
of to economic theory, 30; in
Smith's thought, 25–26. *See also*
economic development; gross
domestic product; gross national
product; national income; production
Wealth of Nations, The (Smith),
21–26, 42, 144
Weigley, Russell, 123